Produced mostly in Athens and London by
VN Gelis during 2015

Dedicated to the millions of Greeks betrayed by the Fake Left

Syriza 'Left' Globalism Implodes

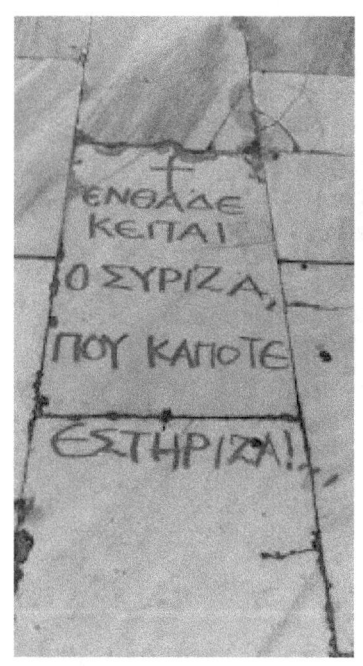

**"Syriza is buried when I once supported it
Sindagma Square 13th July 2015"**

Contents

D. Mass Immigration as a NWO tool of 4th Reich

E. Debates with Pseudo Leftists on Greece

A. Eyewitness Reports: *The Rise of Syriza*

Election 2015 Eyewitness Reports

Introduction

For the first time in a 100 year history the Greek Left fought for state power. Syriza was intransigent in the election of a President in the previous Parliament and the government fell only for Syriza to vote for a President from the Right a few months later and to stay in power with votes from the previous Opposition.

That would imply that Syriza had a pre-assigned role, one that would see it rush through the 3rd Bailout of economic genocide as New Democracy and PASOK couldn't and that is what explains why they insisted on bringing down the previous government. Running on a pre-electoral platform of 'no sacrificies for the Euro' they flipflopped to the position of 'we have no mandate for a break from the Euro' despite tens of thousands being on the streets ready for a break with the Euro. Unable to go Left as they had pre-electoral promises to keep with the Hedge Funds in the City of London, they moved Right.

The debate around the Drachma which started early on during the street protests of 2011 in sections of the non-Globalist left mushroomed to the point where there was 24/7 propaganda about the end of modern civilisation as we know it if it was returned, despite the fact that over 180 countries don't have the Euro and via the referendum the Greeks proved in practice that they aren't afraid of a return of the Euro as the Right campaigned on a slogan of 'Drachma vs Euro' and the whole country heard it.

The articles that follow are in chronological order as to how the debate over the Drachma have developed and some new ones translated which show what is produced in Greece and whether it could survive a transition to the Drachma. Of course this debate isn't really solely about Greece, but about the Euro project as a whole and whether monetary union can last a Grexit.

When E Tsakalotos came to the British Parliament and gave a presentation to British MPs he categorically stated that there is 'no left break from monetary union' 'no progressive solution' there never was a left debate on the topic and all the discussions are from the neofascist right eg Le Pen, Farage etc.

During the first few months Syriza got involved in a lot of modern marketing going on trips to Russia allegedly to get money, sign gas deals, join the BRICS banks etc. This was all a ruse to buy time so the sellout could be marketed appropriately. No single measure apart from re-opening ERT and rehiring a few Economics Ministry cleaners were actually taken. One could argue they were postponed until the negotiations were played out, but they weren't *postponed as there was no intention from day one in implementing anything. Instead of a moratorium of debt repayments Syriza run the coffers dry making capital controls and new agreement inevitable. Instead of a European conference on the Debt we got a Committee under the auspices of the Parliamentary Spokesperson ie not even a parliamentaty committee. Theatrics in the place of politics. In this everyone played their part. Syrizas loyal Left Platform that remained inside Syriza until all the components of the 3rd bailout were voted for. The global media corporates who sold the 'hard left' Syriza campaign and just as they adopted it, they dropped it as if all singing from the same hymn sheet.*

The fools did not understand that the Greek people used Syriza to get rid of PASOK-ND. Syriza brought them back as players when it relied on their support to pass through the 3rd Bailout. But just as political zombies can't be given a new lease of life by a fake left, whatever the outcome of the September elections, implementing the 3rd Bailout of economic genocide will lead to more social conflict and resistance. Syriza came to power on the back of this resistance its implosion signals that parliamentary solutions are nearing their end.

If the Greek labour movement is to survive (what remains of it) without a return to a national currency and some form of controls in the economy (banking, currency, transport, imports etc) Greece will start to fragment and implode. The future will be much worse than the present.

The Capitalist Crisis and the Election of a Syriza Government

US president Lyndon Johnson's hubristic disregard for Greek democracy when he expressed himself with regard to the Greek ambassador's concern with the US's preferred solution on Cyprus: "Then listen to me, Mr Ambassador, fuck your parliament and your constitution. America is an elephant. Cyprus is a flea. If these two fleas continue itching the elephant, they may just get whacked by the elephant's trunk, whacked good ... We pay a lot of good American dollars to the Greeks, Mr Ambassador. If your prime minister gives me talk about democracy, parliament and constitutions, he, his parliament and his constitution may not last very long."

The fact of the matter is that Samaras-ND and Venizelos-PASOK spent the whole of 2014 pretending Grecovery had set in place but no one saw it on the ground. They then went around in the last 3 months stating the Troika is over in Greece and had discussions with Merkel who told them to introduce more cuts until essentially Greece has Chinese wages and zero pensions. Unlike the Latin American caudillos or even those of the ex-satellite states of Russia when the going got tough Samaras and Venizelos chose to cut their leadership short by bringing forward the election of the President by two months instead of bringing about new cuts and creating massive civil unrest and being forced to evacuate by helicopter to ...Miami.

This capitalist crisis is unlike all the other that went before it. What is becoming clear is that it is unrelenting it continues unabated and specifically in Greece it has taken the features of an avalanche. So far 4 political parties have been burnt ND, PASOK, LAOS, Dimar and lets not forget that from 1974 to 2010 the two main parties gained above 85% of the popular vote. In 2012 it had dropped by 50%. This time round it will have easily dropped by another 50% with 3 of the above four political parties disappearing off the political map.

Others who voted for GD and Ind Greeks will also feel that the present govt opens new possibilities for them.... The main losers will be ND PASOK and the KKE from any new election.

KKE-Antarsya electorally working... for New Democracy

Just as Syriza didn't want to govern in 2012 as after all it had no actual programme other than 'end austerity' and remain within the Eurozone, now we have those on the 'left' of Syriza standing independently to weaken its votes so it doesn't get an overall majority. In 2012 the KKE received 4.5% of the vote. It will be a miracly if theya re able to increase it as almost all its political venom is about not voting for Syriza (what Junquer and Schauble have stated already). When in 2012 Tsipras offered a joint slate with the KKE, the KKE responded primarily with such ridiculous arguments that could be summarised in stating they only like to govern with New Democracy or PASOK (which is what they did in 1989). As a result they lost half their votes lost another third when it came to the Euro elections of 2014.

Antarsya whose politics differ not one iota from Syriza but due to the fact that its largest component the SWP-Greece had already split and one of its leaders had gone into Syriza (Davanelos) didn't want to follow the same path as its leaders don't need a career in politics (they have family money as they are related to the ex-central bankster of Greece- Garganas) so they play at politics not with what is required but with what they choose to do. The other coalition partners in Antarsya wanted talks and they are underway with Plan B- Alavanos (ex Sinaspismos chief), Drachma-Katsanevas (ex-PASOK) and EPAM-Kazakis (ex-KKE and Theodorakis) with the aim of a joint slate. In the last elections if their votes had gone over to Syriza it could have matched New Democracy. Now by standing they will be reducing Syrizas electoral prospects if they don't get 3% thereby wasting the vote.

Syrizas Campaign-Not for an Absolute Majority?

During the course of the next month the extent and the style of the Syriza campaign will determine whether they will gain an outright majority. So far they are trying to cook an omelette without breaking any eggs. A difficult task to perform as they are trying to ascertain what the other side are going to do. Germany can refuse everything play hardball and stop all funding to Greece. That will force them out of the Eurozone and in bankruptcy immediately triggering social unrest and revolt. This cannot be a German desire as the whole of the EU project will start to unravel. The Germans cannot expect for Syriza to continue where Samaras left off ie a new round of cuts in wages and pensions

On the other hand does capitalism have anything more to give or is it in a downward spiral where all the gains will now revert to the 19th century? Under these conditions a Syriza victory will only be transitional before something else is born. Just like in the place of PASOK emerged Syriza so with a Syriza victory people will feel they can gain something and demands will emerge in particular around the 30% unemployed and the previous attacks on pensions.

Syriza is a middle class party. It is soft at the edges. It has no real social base in Greek society. It believes that with nice words and correct arguments you can take on the banksters. It will give renewed hope to Greeks to fight and regain a life destroyed by collapsing capitalism. As such it will find it extremely difficult to govern as it can't send out riot police to break up protests like in the Gold mine area of Skouries. If Merkel and Brussels give no leeway they will end up with more militant Greeks and Syriza will be a transitional govt to something far worse for the point of view of the banksters.

The political and economic impasse will be resolved one way or another.

Why was Greece selected?

This is due to the fact that its political class were collaborators with the German 3rd Reich and then went wholly over to Anglo-American imperialism leading Greece into a civil war and a bloodbath which saw a 21% collapse in GDP. Despite only being 2% of the total Eurozone economy Greece was allegedly the sum of all evil the root of all corruption the devil incarnate of what goes wrong when you employ people in the public sector or you have politicians. A nice convenient fairy tale to move the global narrative away from Wall St and the City of London. The corporate media who are an appendage of global capitalism sold the story and it was repeated ad nauseum by Greek and foreign politicians as if working in tandem. If the following course of events is for Greece to be burnt fully and spat out as the example not to follow it is good to heed Aristotles words 'necessity is the mother of invention'. Being forced out of the EZ will enable Greece to print its own money, try to restore some of its control over its economy and leave the EU.

It can then start to trade with Russia and China not the financial parasites who only seek a pound of flesh. What may seem now like a pipedream soon will not. With a resolute leadership that is willing to go into battle the banksters can be defeated. They don't produce much apart from debt and enslavement. The nations of this earth can go back to controlling their destiny not their destiny being decided without them and for them in other corners of the earth forcing them to accept millions of products as well as humans in the free movement of everything which has been called globalization. Economic genocide and the erasure of small nations is what was inaugurated by the 4th Reich in Greece. This time we have a good chance of defeating it like we did with the 3rd. We just need to be willing and creative.

December 2014
VN Gelis

Election Updates January 2015
30th December 2014

Syriza: Will probably get over 35%. The US Ambassador predicted around 44% in a poll they had for themselves according to a mate. Hardly any people are found that won't be voting for Syriza. ND will be forced to get a new leader, many will go over to the Ind Greeks and it will change its name. If Syriza gets an overall majority it will be difficult for Merkel to not seek a compromise. If they boot Greece out of the EZ then the whole EU will unravel in 2015. Greeks can be bought lock stock and barrel and added onto German GDP and funded like the Germans fund their unemployed. If one doesn't vote for Syriza then that implies that you want Samaras to stay in power... The Germans may use an accounting trick to pay the German war reparations to decrease Greece external debt burden thus calling it a one off debt reschedule. The same will not be able to be applied for Italy and Spain. So either Germany adopts Greece or it goes for an abortion. That will unravel the EU faster. The choice is now theirs...

1st January 2015

Syriza has stated that if Merkel does not back down they will call a Referendum. Some people are circulating the FALSE idea that Syriza will continue where Samaras left off. That might be the case with the leadership of Syriza. But if Syriza wanted to continue the same politics they could have voted for President allowed Samaras to run his course and taken a hit with the new round of cuts proposed by the Troika. The fact of the matter is that over 50% of Greeks haven't paid the property tax implemented by the IMF and the so called budget surplus during Grecovery was made up bullshit. That is what is at stake. Thatcher lost the poll tax due to non payment and after a riot almost brought central London into flames. Her successor didn't reintroduce the Poll Tax in the same exact form.

2nd January 2015

Fuchs threatens Greece with expulsion

http://www.telesurtv.net/english/news/Fuchs-Greece-Could-Be-Ousted-from-the-Eurozone-20141231-0008.html

Germany's leadership believe we are in 2012. We are not. The fear of Grexit and the rise of Syriza have existed for 3 years. Same threats do not apply to electorate. Rightwing in Greece grew up in cold war era with tales of the "communists will take your houses (wives, daughters etc.)". Now they complain Samaras is doing it in practice. New Democracy will be unable to hold onto its electoral base and will not find a new one however many votes PASOK or Potami get.

With that in mind empty threats have no meaning. The exit of Greece may not indeed be of a systemic nature to French or German banks but will become a green light that the EU project is unravelling. This is understood clearly by Syriza. So if Germany doesn't bargain they announced a referendum on the debt. Turkeys will never vote for Xmas. Fuchs can go Fuchs himself...

3rd January 2015
Papandreous sets up new mickey mouse organisation called Democratic Socialists.
Will take votes from PASOK and as PASOK is hovering around 3-5% hopefully will do something positive in his life and erase both their chances consigning themselves to the dustbin of history where they belong.

4th January 2015
Syriza held a show of force a controlled Conference in a big auditorium for media consumption. Tsipras tried to do a Blair and control the delegates and who would be assigned to which area as MP's creating a furore at Congress as local organisations did not want candidates jet settled in in particular if they had a murky political past. The Tsipras leadership was defeated in this endeavour. The margin between Samaras and Tsipras keeps on expanding on the corporate controlled media and the figures they provide are of course nonsense. Syriza should easily be in late 30's as a % and Samaras should be below 20%. One needs to remember that in 2012 in the first election the corporate 'public opinion' forming polls gave Syriza 9% and they got double that at 18% and Samaras took previous Presidents vote and almost halved it.

Eyewitness Reports February 2015 Greek Demonstrators in Sindagma Sq

Sindagma Sq- -War of the Roses

15th February
Whilst probably less than last time despite it being on Sunday and with much milder weather the tone was sombre.

No one understands anymore why they are there. There is no longer a reason for demonstrations as Syriza is no longer debating the issue of the Debt, it's folded over on the issue. Most of the banners on demo were saying Not

One Step Back and such were the titles of papers within Syriza - DEA, Marxist Tendency etc.

It's as if last Thursday never happened. Varoufakis was clear in Saturday's interview in the Guardian, there is no Plan B. Separation has occurred, but the divorce hasn't been finalized. Each side is ripping the other side up, like in the film with M Douglas and K Turner in the War of the Roses. Syriza doesn't want to jump and the EU doesn't want to push. This can't go on indefinitely as it implies Greece will have a pay as you go relationship to its debts and everyone else would follow suit. But when you don't have a Plan B and the cash flow dries up you will go the way of the previous four parties under the Troika, into the dustbin of history. If Syriza doesn't cut any deals with Russia like its predecessors, and remains committed to Euroatlanticism it will fracture far quicker than New Democracy. People don't have time to wait for solutions to their problems in the afterlife. Like some leaflets said: *"Better the Drachma than Subjugation, We Don't Owe, We Don't Sell We Don't Pay."*

5th February
The first protest organised via social media occurred on 5th February at 6pm. Thousands arrived possibly around 30k by the time people heard about it. The tone of the mood was that this was the first time since the Squares Movement in June 2011 that people felt free to protest in front of Parliament without a protective barrier or riot police ready to storm and tear gas people.

11th February

The 2nd gathering 11th February was possibly three times the size of Syrizas pre-election rally (around 80-190k) despite the extreme cold and the snow that started falling. People turned up on their own or within organisations. Whilst the mood was sombre many carried Greek flags and sang the national anthem the message was clear, don't back down don't come back with your tail between your legs. A third gathering is scheduled for the final Eurogroup meeting

If Syriza was to just fold and implement Samaras ND policy then there was no reason for the recent elections. The govt would start to fragment as there are already rumblings over Varoufakis statements regarding the % of support to the Troika programme which he placed at 70% in support. If Syriza has no Plan B and is ejected from the Eurogroup then the negotiations were futile.

Merkel's EU Cyprus to Greece
From a Financial to an Electoral Coup

A couple of years back the EU under its alleged attempt at rooting out corruption and financial mismanagement imposed a coup on the Cypriot banking system rendering the economy worthless. Now it has gone another step further rendering the recent Greek elections pointless.

Despite the massive swing to parties of the fake Left in Greece around 2.5m votes and despite the minimal reformist programme trying to arrest the downward spiral of austerity it was not meant to be.

Less than one month in power Syriza was forced to succumb to the 4th Reich. Its pre-electoral propaganda about Debt writedown, increasing the minimum wage to Euro 751, increasing state pensions by a month up to E700, bringing in a min tax threshold of Euro 12k and removing the hated 'haratsi' property tax appear to all have gone out of the window. The difficult task will be how to manage the expectations of the voters who have been crushed by the economic genocide programme adopted by the Troika (IMF, ECB, EU).

The unrelenting capitalist crisis which has become exarcebated by the creation of the Eurozone whereby economic giants like Germany are in the same bed as semi-industrialised Greece has led to the creation of the EUs first debt colony. Under guise of saving the Greeks from debt the Germans have reduced them to penury. In this they have form. In the 19th century their colonial invasions of Africa were made to end black slavery in order to inaugurate colonial slavery for their geopolitical interests primarily resources which Germany didn't produce but required for their industrial giants.

Despite four large demonstrations (1) in many cities of Greece against the EU's dictat's the wishes of the Greek population have no place within the EU. They cannot have any alternative programme that attempts to resolve the glaring contradictions of collapsing capitalism. There is no humanitarian crisis, there aren't millions of unemployed who aren't sent tax demands and the 4 million people who are in debt to Inland Revenue have as a threat if they own property to lose their homes via forced repossessions 8,000 Greeks haven't committed suicide, children don't go to school and faint from hunger. This in a nutshell is Schauble's line. In the last five years Greek banks have received E233 billion in bailouts and these costs have been born by the massive reduction in wages and pensions (between 30-50%). Continuing along this path means that the widening budget deficit have to have inbuilt cuts according to the Memorandum of Understanding agreements signed with the Troika. It was these agreements Syriza was allegedly going to rip up and destroy once in power. (2)

According to the Wall StreetJournal Greece (3) has Euro E29billion commitments this year and without new loans they can't service these commitments. Greeks owe around Euro70b to the state and that represents around 3.8m people and 400k businesses. That does not include mortgage debt, bank loans. In total Greece's foreign debts are around E325b and other debts around E300-350b so in total around E650b. The debt write off has gone through the stage whereby an opposition came to power expressing what is actually going on the ground but now has to collect the debts wearing a 'left' lapel. The issue though remains that changing a label from hard right (ND) to radical left (Syriza) does not debts collect. Blood cannot come out of a stone. With 2m unemployed and probably another 1m underemployed (out of an official 4.5m workers) and underpaid severely the economy for the majority of people has been destroyed, it no longer services the needs of the Greek nation. Tourism and agriculture still provide the main source of income with exports being reduced since last year (whilst tourism saw growth), but the nature of the globalised economy imply that any gains in those areas aren't translated into jobs for the domestic market as a large slice of the labour force in both these industries are non-unionised immigrant labour who are paid in cash and even with a minimum export of Euro50 a month to their families in Asia can be paid anything, if at all.

Unable to truly negotiate, Syriza thought they could convince the Eurogroup on a wing and a prayer, (or was it the Greek electorate?) talk about the Debt in general and then drop it in two days like Varoufakis did. Why would the EU write off Greek debts when the total EU debts are more than E13trillion? What makes Greek debts special or different? Any agreement on Greek debts would immediately open the floodgates for all else, Italy, Spain, Portugal etc. Even if the debts were zeroed the same debts would accrue again if the nature of the economic relationships don't change. When you have an open market in services, trade, capital and labour, lilliputian Greece cannot compete with heavy industrial goods from Germany or cheap goods from China or agricultural goods from Africa. The economy becomes absolutely dependent on debt servicing when exports cannot be produced to be sold as each industry has been successfully shut down (cloth making, shoe making, ship repairs etc) In other words there can be no national economic policy by extension national elections. Brussels decides.

For Syriza to survive it has to go Left if it does not want to go the way of its previous four predecessors in the IMF period (LAOS, Dimar, PASOK, ND). Trade with Russia direct. Offer a naval base to them to guard the country from neighbours attacks. Agree to the Russian pipeline to be stationed on the Greek-Turkish border. Ensure strategic industries are still in the control of the state: ports, electricity, water, transport etc. Abolish the Dublin 2 agreements whereby illegal immigrants are dumped in Greece as it is a border country of the EU and it clearly does not have the capacity to cope with hundreds of thousands of new arrivals. Enforce a policy of 'less work but work for all' with no loss of pay. Seriously argue for Default of Debts which have been paid back at least three time over and if that does not occur exit the EZ and go for the Drachma with an exit from the EU. Without taking these measures there will be no economic policy that isn't dictated directly by Brussels. Brussels agenda is to create a tax free export processing zone that can compete directly with Asia in the region formally known as Greece with E300 wages and non-existent pensions or (just private) healthcare. That agenda remains intact despite the provisional time out by the election of Syriza.

21st February 2015

Notes

1. Eyewitness Reports from the Demos against the Eurogroup:
http://imfoccupationgreece.blogspot.gr/2015/02/eyewitnes
s-reports-sindagma-sq-war-of.html
2. The Economics of Genocide by the IMF
http://imfoccupationgreece.blogspot.gr/2015/01/the-
economics-of-genocide-made-in.html
3. WSJ-Greek Debt Commitments 2015
http://www.enikonomia.gr/economy/15002,WSJ:_Ti_prep
ei_na_plhrwnei_ka8e_mhnah_E.html

New Democracy politicians bloodied during the 2011
protests. 3rd Bailout will bring these developments back

Syriza, The View From Within: Glezos, Kouvelakis Lapavitsas

M Glezos on the Agreement 20th February 2015

First major negative reaction against the Eurogroup agreement from inside SYRIZA comes from Manolis Glezos, Member or European Parliament of SYRIZA, and a living legend of the Resistance against fascism (in 1941 along with Lakis Santas they took down the German flag from the Acropolis)
Here is a rough translation of his statement
Statement by Manolis Glezos
...
Before it is too late
The fact that the Troika has been renamed 'the institutions', the Memorandum has been renamed the 'Agreement' and the Creditors have been renamed the 'Partners', in the same manner as baptizing meat as fish, does not change the previous situation.
And you can't change the vote of the Greek People at the January 25 election.
The Greek people voted what SYRIZA promised: that we abolish the regime of austerity that is the strategy of not only the oligarchies of Germany and the other creditor countries but also of the Greek oligarchy; that we abrogate the Memoranda and the Troika and all the austerity legislation; That the next day with one law we abolish the Troika and its consequences.

A month has passed and this promise has yet to become action.
It is a pity indeed

From my part I APOLOGIZE to the Greeκ people for having assisted in this illusion
Before the wrong direction continues
Before it is too late, let's react
Above all the members, the friends and supporters of SYRIZA, in urgent meetings at all levels of the organization have to decide if they accept this situation.

Some people say that in an agreement you must also make some concessions. By principle between the oppressor and the oppressed there can be no compromise, as there can be no compromise between the slave and the conqueror; Freedom is the only solution.

But even if accept this absurdity, the concessions that have already been made by the previous pro-memoranda government with unemployment, poverty and suicide, are beyond any limit of concession...

Manolis Glezos, Brussels 22-2-2015

On Syriza and the Retreat...

In the last few days there have been two sophisms circulating among those who refuse to look reality square in the face and recognise the retreat that Syriza has been forced to make, as well as its possible consequences. Or rather, two and a half. And I say 'forced' with good reason, because the new government has been trapped by its mistaken strategy: though I wouldn't say it was a 'betrayal' or 'capitulation', since these are moralising terms that are of very little use for understanding political processes.

The first sophism: 'Syriza has no mandate to quit the Eurozone'. If it had adopted such a position it wouldn't have won the elections. Putting it that way, we see how absurd this reasoning is. Yes, of course, it had no 'mandate to quit the Eurozone'. But it certainly didn't have a 'mandate' to abandon the core of its programme in order to hang onto the Euro, either! And, without doubt, if it had presented itself to the electorate saying 'here's our programme, but if we find that its implementation is incompatible with keeping the Euro then we'll forget about it', then it wouldn't have achieved much success at the polls. For good reason: keeping the Euro AT ANY COST is exactly the same fundamental argument as the pro-Memorandum parties who've ruled Greece all these years put forward. And even if Syriza never fully clarified its position on the Euro, it did always reject the logic of 'the euro at any price'. On that note, let's remember that contrary to what most commentators think, Syriza's programmatic texts do not rule out leaving the Eurozone if forced to by the Europeans' intransigence, or defaulting on the debt payments. Though it is true that recently these texts seem to have been rather hidden away.

A second variant of this first sophism: Syriza had a dual mandate of breaking with austerity AND staying in the Euro. This sounds more rational than the first version, but nonetheless it is still sophistry. It's as if the two sides of this mandate were equally important and thus it would be politically legitimate, if we had to choose (and indeed we do have to choose – that's precisely the problem), to sacrifice the break with austerity on the altar of keeping the Euro. Without having even abandoned its mandate! But then why not turn that reasoning the other way around, saying 'since I realise the two objectives are incompatible, I choose to stick to the break with austerity, since essentially that is the reason why Greeks voted for a party of the radical Left'? That is, to opt for the rupture and not 'stability' within the existing framework. We might at least think that this choice is more befitting of a radical Left party that sets 'socialism' as its 'strategic goal' (even if that clearly wasn't the agenda on which it won the elections).

The third sophism is the one **promoted** by **Étienne Balibar** and Sandro Mezzadra. Having sarcastically remarked on those on the 'left wing of Syriza' who are crying 'capitulation' (let's ignore for now the fact that no one on the Syriza left has ever used these terms), from recent events Balibar and Mezzadra draw the conclusion that 'we will not be able to build a politics of freedom and equality in Europe simply by asserting national sovereignty'. According to them, the main thing is that Syriza has bought time, admittedly at the cost of making some concessions (with the obligatory reference to Lenin to prove the radicalism of what they're arguing); and that it has allowed for other future political victories (they mention Spain) and the development of social movement mobilisations of a 'transnational' bent (the likes of Blockupy).

Here again we are swimming in the waters of sophistry – of a pseudo-naivety that would be confusing, if it did not make total sense coming from ardent defenders of the 'European project' (a 'nice version' of it, of course) like these two authors. After all, the rhythms of the political forces to which they refer are not in synchrony. From now until summer the Greek government faces a series of more than pressing deadlines; and it's hard to see how a successful demonstration in Frankfurt, or even the possibility of Podemos winning the Spanish elections at the end of the year, could change the situation in Syriza's favour. The gaps among these different forces' temporal rhythms are one of the reasons why the national context is of such strategic importance to the actors in the political struggle: it is the terrain where the power relations among classes are condensed in decisive fashion.

Balibar and Mezzadra also gravely underestimate the demobilising effect that will inevitably follow – both within Greece and at the European level – from the perception that Greece and the Syriza government have been forced to kowtow to the EU's austerity diktats. And this what everyone is ultimately going to think, whatever the short-sighted defenders of the Greek government do to try and dress it up differently. Already in Greece, the climate of mobilisation and rediscovered confidence that we saw in the first weeks after the election now seems long in the past. Of course, the mobilisations may well resume, but this time they will be directed against the government's decisions, and in any case they won't appear 'on demand'.

Making any political choice conditional on the emergence of social movements is more than risky. It is a way of saying that it is a decision that will have to be changed if the mobilisations do not take place or if they are insufficiently powerful. In reality, we have to take the opposite line of march. We have to assume that we have already made the decision to break with austerity: it's this that stimulates mobilisation, which will then enjoy (or acquire) its own autonomy. Moreover, that is exactly what happened in Greece during the government's 'confrontation' with the EU between 5 and 20 February, when tens of thousands of people took to the street in a largely spontaneous manner, outside of any party framework.

Besides, the argument that 'we have won some time' is in this case an illusion, since during these four months of supposed 'respite', Syriza will in fact be forced to operate within the existing framework. And this will strengthen this framework: Syriza will have to implement a good part of what the Troika (now restyled 'the institutions') demands, while 'putting off' the application of the key measures of its own programme – precisely the policies that would have allowed it to 'make a difference' and cement the social alliance that brought it to power. Indeed there is a very major risk that the time that Syriza has 'won' will prove to have been 'wasted time', undermining

Syriza's base while allowing its enemies (particularly those on the far Right) to regroup and present themselves as the only partisans of a 'real systemic break'.

We should also note that, despite the disgust that Europeanism addicts like Balibar and Mezzadra feel upon any mention of 'the national', the very political successes to which they refer, from Syriza to Podemos, not only took place within a national context – changing the relations of force precisely insofar as they allow radical Left political movements to access the nation state's levers of power – but were also, in part, only possible thanks to these parties' insistence on national sovereignty: in a democratic, popular, non-nationalist sense, open to the outside world. 'National-popular' discourse and references to 'patriotism' abound – Tsipras and Iglesias are perfectly willing to use these terms – as do national flags (Greek and Spanish Republican ones, not to mention the flags of the nationalities within the Spanish State) among the crowds and the 'autonomous' movements (as Mezzadra and Balibar call them) filling these countries' streets and town squares.

More than anything else, this shows that in the particular case of the dominated countries on the periphery of Europe like Spain and Greece, reference to 'the national' is a terrain of struggle that progressive forces have managed to hegemonise, thus making it one of the most powerful factors driving their success. And this is the basis on which we can build a real internationalism, not the empty talk –

entirely disconnected from the concrete realities of political struggle – about a supposedly already-existing and unmediated 'European' or 'transnational' terrain.

One last point, to conclude: there is a degree of truth in the first two sophisms, when they talk about Syriza's 'mandate' to leave the Eurozone. It is indeed true that there has been a contradiction in the party's dominant approach to this question, a contradiction that has now burst into full view. The idea of breaking with austerity and Greece's debt burden within the existing European framework could not have been more clearly refuted in reality. In such a situation, it is vital that we speak frankly and honestly. The first thing to do is to admit the failure, and thus the need for us to discuss once again the best strategy for Syriza to keep its promises and get Greece out of its current rut. At the same time, this will send a message of struggle to all those people – and there are a lot of them – who were counting on the 'hope offered by Greece' and rightly refuse to accept that they are beaten.
London, 25 February 2015
BY *Stathis Kouvelakis*

The Syriza strategy has come to an end

In a joint interview with German daily Der Tagesspiegel and ThePressProject International, Syriza MP and economist Costas Lapavitsas says that the time has come for Greece and its partners to understand that "they are flogging a dead horse". Instead, they should work together on "an exit that will be negotiated and consensual". The first step? "After 5 years of scaremongering and misinformation, there has to be at last a genuine push.

By Elisa Simantke and Nikolas Leontopoulos

It is not new that Costas Lapavitsas, professor at SOAS in London, has been actively advocating Grexit – though this is the first time he does so since he was elected MP with Syriza in January 2015. His views were once again shunned not only by political opponents but also by ministers of his own party.

However, even if one disagrees with Lapavitsas's ideas about the currency, it's hard to dismiss his assessment - confirmed from developments in the past few weeks - that the Eurozone doesn't seem to allow any real middle way between austerity and a Grexit: "The leadership of the party knows that it has a very tough choice ahead of it: Do we persevere with the programme that we proclaimed to the Greek people? Or do we submit to what the institutions, the Brussels Group, the troika, whatever you want to call it, want us to do? These two things are incompatible."

His two recent interviews with 'Bild' newspaper in Germany and 'Jacobin' magazine in the US triggered a flurry of reactions in Greece: «A plan of folly with drachma and gas rationing!» (link in Greek) titled 'moderate' TOC, followed by similar headlines in country's most media.

How wise is it for a debate that has been dominating the columns of the world's newspapers and the plenaries of the continent's parliaments to remain a taboo in the country it mostly concerns? No matter whether Grexit would ultimately be a catastrophic strategy or "the only logical solution", the point conveyed through this joint interview to Berlin daily Der Tagesspiegel and ThePressProject International is that, "there has to be a genuine public debate at last".

What's your opinion on the negotiations so far? How is the government doing?

The Syriza strategy has been - and it remains - that a change in the political alignment of forces in Greece, in Europe, or generally, would act as a catalyst in the Eurozone. This strategy has now come to an end. The real question is how long it will be before people understand it.

I was always extremely skeptical of it. I always argued that it isn't just about political alignment, there are institutional mechanisms and the logic of the monetary union. And those who believe that a simple change of politics is enough to transform this, were mistaken and I think this has been confirmed.

What we've seen is that the institutional framework of the Eurozone and the ideological machinery attached to it are not susceptible to arguments that come from electoral realignments. So the agreement of the 20th of February at the Eurogroup reflects that.

Do your party members notice that this strategy has come to an end?

Syriza is a big organization which has grown very rapidly. It reflects society. It isn't some kind of traditional party of the left, and therefore there is a variety of opinions and of political conscience.

I think that the leadership of the party knows that it has a very tough choice ahead of it: Do we persevere with the programme that we proclaimed to the Greek people? Or do we submit to what the institutions, the Brussels Group, the troika, whatever you want to call it, want us to do? These two things are incompatible.

So there is no middle way?

There is no middle way. The Eurozone will not allow it. Do I think the leadership was surprised? Yes, I suspect they were to a certain extent. Because my reading of the situation is that the leadership genuinely believed that you could change the political alignments, you could change electoral arithmetic, and on this basis change Europe, change European policies.

So what should the Greek government do in your opinion?

Greece needs to consider the true alternative path which is to leave this failed monetary union. It is clearly the only way that was there from the beginning – which is basically exit. If you are going to apply such a programme, as Syriza has proclaimed, which is not radical – Syriza's programme is just moderate Keynesianism -, you need to think seriously of how you are going to get out of the confines of the Eurozone.

Do you think Syriza has the mandate for it?

A straight answer is no. Syriza has a mandate to fulfil its programme. Indirectly, not directly, it has a mandate to keep the country in the Eurozone. But this question was never openly posed to the Greek people.

Is the solution a referendum?

The first thing to do is not so much discuss the idea of a referendum but actually that of the alternative strategy. There has to be a genuine public debate at last. That's not easy because for five years this country has been subjected to the most incredible misinformation and scaremongering campaigns. So the atmosphere has been very badly poisoned. It is not impossible to have this debate now but it is much more difficult than a few years back.

In my judgement, the best strategy right now is what I call a consensual and orderly exit. Not a contested exit.

Can you elaborate on that?

I think Greece should set a target for itself to negotiate an exit basically without rupture, without falling out, without fighting, without unilateral actions. This would mean: Exit takes place and Greece seeks deep debt restructuring.

Q: Why would the EU-partners accept? This exit has two elements that the EZ doesn't want: the exit itself and the debt restructuring.

I am not entirely certain the EZ doesn't want exit. I suspect that it does. And in my judgement if a country asked for a negotiated way out, it might as well receive in it. Germany, Schauble, back in 2011 was in favor of a negotiated exit.

The price for the EZ should be debt restructuring. But they are two more very important elements: the protection of the exchange rate and protection of the banks. These are essentially costless for the ECB because Greece is a small country.

What would Europe win out of it?

Peace and quiet. (Pause…) For a period.

Why only for a period?

Because the monetary union in my judgement is a major historical failure. It's Europe's biggest failure in decades. And it will not last. But obviously it might last long enough for Greece to be dead. Of course the EZ proponents believe it is going to last forever. It is a historical delusion. Monetary unions don't last this long. Let them believe it. Fine.

Would the EU as a political construction survive if countries exit the monetary union?

In 15 years the monetary union has undone all the goodwill generated in Europe by the EU. The state of relations in the European countries today is probably worse than it's been for decades. The state of affairs between Germany and Greece is appalling, absolutely atrocious. And this because of the euro.

This is proof that this money doesn't generate solidarity, this money creates divisions. And this is again the biggest evidence of its failure. Now stubbornness, unwillingness to recognize the failure of it in the last five years is making things worse. What the EU has done in the last 5 years is to tie itself even more closely around the common currency instead of deeply restructuring it. It has actually made it harder. So yes if now the common currency fails, which I think it will, then the EU will be in question, that's the price to pay for the historical mistake of the common currency.

So for Greece, does leaving the EZ also mean leaving the EU?

The most important is to differentiate between the EU and the EZ. In this country, and in most of Europe, a sustained confusion has been going on for years. That the membership of one equals the membership of the other. It's of course absurd because there are members of the EU which are not members of the European monetary union. If Greece leaves the euro, it doesn't have to leave the EU at the same time. If the Greek people want to leave the EU, let them leave the EU. But that's a separate question. This conflation has been deadly and it's been used ideologically...

GERMANY IS THE MOST DELINQUENT COUNTRY

There were binding mechanisms even before the monetary union...

The previous regimes were not successful but, compared to the disaster the common currency has been, the previous regimes were beacons of success. The bottom line: Europe needs a monetary system that allows for monetary flexibility. It is complete nonsense to impose a system of monetary inflexibility and at the same time to create flexibility through labour markets and the private sector. Butthe most profound reason for the failure of the euro is of course German policy.

Why that?

Germany is the country that is the most delinquent in Europe. Not Greece, not Spain, not Italy. And certainly not France. France is playing far more by the book than Germany. Germany has been not keeping the rules and I can make it very simple for you: Germany often accuses Greece - Schauble for instance does - that Greece has been living beyond its means. It's true. But Germany has also been systematically living below its means, and this is how exports are generated, not because of technology, productivity and all that. That's why it is so successful.

But when you are in a monetary union it cannot be a bad thing to live above your means and a good thing to live below. The real rule must be to live by your means. So Germany has not kept the rules and the price is paid by the German people. I understand full well how the German people live. I know very well that wages have not risen for years, that one third of the labor force lives under precarious conditions. Precarious employment, wages below productivity...,

So what you are saying is that the euro has not been good for the German people either...

This also explains why the German people are annoyed and angry when it comes to sending money abroad, paying for others. Of course, I would be angry too in that position: you live in a very tight way, you count your beans and then somebody comes and tells you, you have to pay.

On the other hand, German exporting business, the German banks, this is a different story. They 've done very well. But that's for the German people to sort out.

Do you think the Germans are kept in fear with a purpose? If you are a German you are always told "things will get worse". Germany – we are told- is not performing as it could, Europe is not performing as it could, there is China, there is India, the globalization...

Globalization is one of those words that means all and nothing. There has been a consistent policy on the part of the German establishment to scare the German public and the German workers, to keep them in fear of tomorrow and of unemployment in particular, there is no doubt. The original idea back in 1998-1999 when unemployment was high is that we accept low wages to restore employment within the confines of a monetary union. Now the argument seems to be 'we accept low wages to compete with the Chinese'. There is no end to this. The truth is low wages are not good for Germany. Germany needs a policy of boosting domestic demand. This is neo-mercantilism, the belief that growth comes from abroad only, that the only wealth is exports.

A THREE-STAGE PLAN FOR GREECE

Are you making the same point about Greece? Is domestic demand the key to return to growth? How should Greece get back on its feet?

There are three stages. First, as I said, is the negotiated, consensual, orderly exit.

Second stage is recovery and that would depend very much on recovery of domestic demand which is very heavily repressed in this country. There are vast resources lying unused. Small and medium enterprises would be reactivated, that's what would really restart the Greek economy. Not exports - this worship of exports is nonsense.

But obviously that is not really a path for sustainable growth. What Greece would need after that would be an industrial policy to restructure its productive base, to integrate itself in the world economy on a different basis. That would take a few years.

But Greece would be still part of a common market, as a member of the EU. So it is not so easy to go back to domestic demand and to the SMEs, because it would have to kick out the big companies that could still sell cheaper.

I believe that Greece could out-compete imports very easily. Unfortunately, wages have been destroyed during the last 5 years due to bailout policies. A devaluation of 15-20% (but no more since as I said the ECB would defend the exchange rate) would give a tremendous competitive advantage. Wages would then gradually rise again.

What are the chances for that to happen? For Greece to choose that path?

At 2010 I said there are 3 possible solutions. Austerity, 'the good euro' and exit. I said that the most likely solution would be austerity and this would be a disaster. As for the good euro strategy (i.e., that you achieve Keynesian policy within the confines of the euro – the strategy of Syriza), I said that the chances of this occurring were close to zero. The strategy of exit is the only logical one. The real issue is will it be contested or orderly? I don't know. But exit there will be at some point.

THE POISONOUS IDEOLOGY OF 'EUROPEANISM'

Q: How can it be orderly when now even implying that the negotiations are not going well brings panics and fear of a bank run?

The first thing to happen is for the EU and Greece to understand that they are flogging a dead horse. After 5 years of torture, it is time to finish. This strategy has come to an end. Some sense please. So when I say a strategic aim this is what I mean. People have to come to terms with it. And those who refuse to see, it is because of ideological reasons, because this ideology is poisoning the debate.

What is this ideology?

It is not neoliberalism, it is Europeanism. The idea of Europe as this transcendental entity which is good for all of us and we all belong to it. This great fiction that has emerged in the dominant countries and has come to penetrate the weaker countries.

I am socialist, old style, with the old meaning of the word, the idea of the United States of Europe and of European solidarity is a socialist idea and I share it. Obviously it has also been a Nazi idea, used by Hitler. No one has the monopoly of the idea of a unified Europe.

I don't believe in a single European people, there is no European demos, and there shouldn't be. Europe is about plurality, many different languages, cultures. Since when was it desirable for all of us to be just European, to be one thing?

These are illusions and ideologies. I don't see a political convergence, I see the rise of fascism, the rise of the extreme right, I see extreme tension. Front National in France is at 30% of the vote, and the way things are going, I would not be surprised if the next president of France were a fascist.

If the euro was such a bad idea, why is there this "stubbornness" - as you called it - across Europe to support it? What are the interests behind the idea?

Money is the embodiment of non-economic relations as well. It embodies social relations, it has identity attached to it. This often means national identity. The Americans are the dollar, the British are the pound, the Germans used to be the Deutsche Mark. The euro particularly in the countries of the periphery has come to mean being European. You see it also in the Baltic countries. So there is an element of identity and an element of international policy.

But why the core countries of the EU are so much attached to the idea of the common currency?

I think the core doesn't know how to get out. A bad mistake was made 15 years ago, and the risks of getting out are perceived as very high. At the same time, some special interests, the exporting sector, the banking sector, are strongly defending it because it has served their strategy.
Costas Lapavitsas

Syriza **The View from Abroad:**

Greece: Pressue on Syriza to Deliver
Leo Garib

GAZING across Sytagma Square at the Greek parliament, Despina Kostopoulou explained why her country's future is hanging in the balance. The 53 year-old office cleaner is not part of Greece's new Syriza government, which is locked in a titanic battle with Europe's big powers. She's not, in fact, a politician at all. But as a leader of one of the most important Greek protests in the last few years, she knows what needs to be done to save her country.

Greece's new left-leaning Syriza government are eyeball to eyeball with Germany, the European Union (EU), the European Central Bank (ECB), and the International Monetary Fund (IMF). And Greeks have been pouring onto the streets to support Syriza. In Athens, thousands have been packing Syntagma Square urging Syriza to keep its promises and scrap the spending cuts, privatisations and attacks on workers' rights which have brought Greece to its knees after being forced on the country by the EU, the ECB and IMF.

In the high-stakes diplomacy, Germany, the EU and the ECB are threatening to bankrupt Greece if it ditches the austerity programme. Syriza warns it will quit the

Eurozone of countries using the Euro if it's not allowed to reverse austerity and invest in jobs and living standards. That could spark a global financial meltdown. The only way to make sure Syriza doesn't blink first is for Greeks to show their muscle and pour onto the streets, warns Despina.

"Syriza got to power because Greek workers came out onto the streets to support it and put it into power and now we need to keep coming onto the streets to keep it in power," she said. "If we come onto the streets when Syriza is renegotiating the national debt, and if we come onto the streets when Syrizia looks like it might not deliver its promises – and sometimes it won't, then things will get better and we'll win. The future of our country depends on what we do now. It's up to us, more than ever."

Despina is one of the thousands of sacked government workers who have been promised their job back by Syriza. A cleaner for the ministry of finance for more than 20 years, she was one of 595 laid off without warning by the last government. She helped lead a 16-month strike, which won the support of Greeks and captured media attention around the world.

As she spoke, she pointed to a display of photographs of the strike. Image after image showed the cleaners – plainly dressed middle-aged women – being manhandled and beaten by armour-clad riot police. In some, the women are being treated for serious injuries and in one, Despina is being carried to safety, her face disfigured and swollen.

"It was just announced on the morning television news that we would be fired. I went to sleep a worker and woke up unemployed," she recalled. "That's the way it was then. Workers' rights were ignored or cancelled by the government. Now we're going back to work and that's important for us and our families. But the most important issue isn't us returning to work, it is for us to help change the whole situation in Greece."

Even before the strike, the cleaners' wages had plunged as Greece went into economic meltdown under the austerity programme. After the overnight announcement their jobs were under review as a prelude to redundancy their wages slashed again and the cleaners found themselves on the breadline.

"My family supported me but if it wasn't for my partner, I would have been on the street," said Despina, whose wages were cut to just 400 euros-a-month. "But I was one of the lucky ones. Some women were getting less than 300 euros-a-month because they hadn't worked at the ministry as long as me. They owed so much in rent they were going days without food just to keep their home and were fainting from exhaustion. Some lost their homes and had to move in with their families, some had children who had to quit their studies. It was a social catastrophe. We were kept going because in every area we were supported by solidarity networks, giving us clothes, food and medical help." That even included children who made soap from olives to raise money for the cleaners.

A political awakening for the women, their strike also won the backing of millions of Greeks fed up with austerity.

"I was never involved in politics on this level before and it's been huge for me to have taken part in this struggle," said Despina, who regularly slept on the 24-hour picket line outside the ministry in Athens, and was among the strikers invited to speak at anti-austerity protests across Europe. "Not many of us had the chance to go to university but we learned a lot in that struggle, it was a real education. It has shown me how strong the Greek people can be and why we need to keep going."

The scars of the austerity economics are everywhere. In Athens, shops are boarded up and walls daubed with angry political graffiti, while the sight of a mother and her children scavenging in bins for food no longer turns heads. For some the unprecedented decline is simply too much and suicide rates have rocketed.

After five years of austerity, the economy has shrunk by at least 25%, unemployment has soared to almost 2 million and millions more work only a few days a year and among young Greeks the jobless rate is at least 50%. Employers were given a green light to hire workers from Eastern Europe, Asia and Africa on low wages. State-owned assets were sold cheaply amid a storm of corruption scandals. Pensions have been slashed and there has been a bonfire of workers' rights and social protection. Hospitals and clinics have been shut while doctors and nurses run volunteer services, sometimes using veterinary equipment. Stripped of unemployment insurance, millions of Greeks rely on soup kitchens or the charity of their families.

Greek author and political commentator VN Gelis said if Syriza is to survive it simply must ditch the hated austerity programme and deliver on its promises to invest in the country.

"If Syriza just folds and continues implementing the policies of the last government, even some kind of austerity-light programme, then there would have been no point in the elections last month," he said. "Voters completely turned their backs on the old parties of Pasok and New Democracy, which traditionally formed governments. They rejected them for implementing policies forced on Greece by the EU – in particular Germany, the ECB and the IMF, known collectively as the Troika and hated by Greeks. For Syriza to go back to those same policies would be to completely ignore the will of the Greek people, to deny the election, and condemn Syriza to the dustbin of history. Syriza would simply fragment into the different groups that came together to form the party."

And he expects Greeks to go on packing Syntagma Square, piling the pressure on Syriza. He continued: "There have already been rumblings over statements by Syriza's finance minister Yanis Varoufakis over his alleged statements agreeing to implement some of the Troika's austerity programme in exchange for a cash injection. I saw tens of thousands packing Syntagma Square calling on Syriza not to make that kind of deal." But, he warned, Syriza will need a "workable Plan B" in the event it is ejected from the Eurozone. Like a growing number of Greeks, Van Gelis would welcome a return to Greece's old currency, the Drachma, and more trade with Russia and China.

The biggest China deal is also one of the most controversial, however. The sale of part of the Piraeus shipyard to a Chinese industrial giant was a main plank of the austerity economics. But it was bitterly opposed by many Greeks, including the shipyard workers who warned against lower wages and the dilution of labour rights.

Now the deal is back under the microscope with development minister Panyiotis Lafazanis suggesting the last government's plans for a privatisation of the rest of the shipyard may be reviewed, a position in line with Syriza policy. In the background, Beijing has been lobbying for Cosco, Washington pressing for a US giant to be given the port and Germany and the EU for Greece to stick to the austerity policy of privatisations. The battle over Piraeus illustrates exactly the kind of difficulty Syriza faces as its anti-austerity pledges come face to face with realpolitik, said Van Gelis.

The docks are in Piraeus, an industrial area just a short train ride from Athens. The metro trains serving Piraeus are older and dirtier than those running through the rest of Athens, and as they slip through the suburbs, past the home of Greek football champions Olympiakos and into solidly working class districts, the stations and the streets show the scars of decay. By the time the trains reach Piraeus, the evidence of decline is everywhere. Struggling hotels offering rock bottom discounts, migrant workers hawking cheap goods, and everywhere in its narrow streets the jobless and penniless scour bins with specially adapted hooks, or huddle near markets waiting for leftover food.

The largest port in the Mediterraneam, Piraeus had been the jewel in Greece's industrial crown. Its decline began in the 1980s with the imposition of EU free trade rules but it has been utterly devastated by the social and industrial blitzkrieg of the last five years.

In 2010, half the port was sold for 500 million euros to Chinese state-owned Cosco – a record foreign investment in Greece but a snip for the shipping giant with plans to open a new Silk Route to Europe.

The Cosco-owned Pier II is humming with activity. Towering cranes heave giant containers off the ships, trucks weave down roadways. Business has risen three-fold since the privatisation.

But it has come at a heavy price. The EU parliament was warned Cosco has imposed sweatshop conditions, trying to ban union membership among its workforce of more than 500. Reports surfaced of workers earning less than half the wages paid to those in the neighbouring Greek state-owned pier, of workers being forced to gruelling eight-hour shifts without a break for food or to use the bathroom, and of exhausted workers on 24-hour, seven day-a-week standby for shift work at the risk of losing their jobs. Workers reported taking containers into their vehicles to urinate in.

"The privatisation has accelerated the race to the bottom – a sharp deterioration of conditions, union-bashing and the under-cutting of labour protection," said Yannis Deliyannis, local official of the dock workers union, OMYLE.

The union office is a converted container at the entrance to the state-owned pier. Inside, its walls are plastered with posters demanding an end to austerity, warning against the rise of Greek fascism and for the country to quit the EU.

But the state-owned pier is a shadow of its old self. The tarmac is cracked and in places swims with stagnant water. Small groups of men are at work but the towering cranes stand idle, the wind whistling through their rusting cantilevers.

In the last 30 years, the number working in the dockyards has plunged from 25,000 to fewer than 2,500, with just 500 working on any day. The work is shared out, meaning most work fewer than 30 days a year, explained Deliyannis. Just 10% of workers reach the threshold of 50 days of work a year to qualify for free state health care. And with workers paid between 75 and 125 euros for a seven-hour day, they are struggling to reach the breadline.

"This was once a beautiful shipyard with enough work for us all to live but the EU has systematically taken the work. Now we just can't survive," added Deliyannis. "Now workers have to rely on their family or their parents, if their parents are pensioners. Families are breaking up because of the economic crisis, people are committing suicide and homes are being repossessed."
The union has also found itself thrust into the battle against the effects of austerity in the communities where its members live. When the last government introduced laws making it easier to seize people's homes, the local union helped organise protests to physically confront officials.

"We can't just fight for ourselves now, we have to fight for the communities too," continued Deliyannis. "Our job is to protect all workers – to stop repossessions, stop electricity from being cut-off. We are organising to stop the policies of economic genocide. And we will organise against the Syriza government, if we have to. We will demand a rational economic plan under which the state will intervene to rebuild the ports and rebuild the economy, and restore worker's rights. Greece is a shipping nation so we want proper rights for workers, regular work, health and safety rules, health cover and laws to stop people working too many hours. We are wary the Syriza government will continue along the same path as the previous governments and if they do, we will organise to stop them. But if they do things that are good for us, if they keep their promises, we'll support them all the way."

Nearby a statue of a ship worker – muscular and defiant – appears to survey the wreckage of the docks. Underneath it a small knot of men share a cigarette, their hands in their pockets, their collars turned up against the wind.

One, a welder in his late 50s with a battered face and the gait of an old boxer, has been out of work for five years. He preferred not to give his name and said the union has not done enough to confront austerity and said he voted Syriza. He lives in Perama, a suburb of Piraeus, with three children who are also jobless. They survive on food hand-outs. His wife recently died, he confided.

"We have no money, no pensions, no health care," he said. "All we have are the solidarity clinics for basic food. I have friends who have divorced because of the pressure. Some people commit suicide. But the communities have tried to support each other. There hasn't been an increase in crimes and we've organised to stop people having their electricity cut for not paying taxes or having their homes repossessed. A lot of people feel Syriza is our last hope, and we'll fight like hell to stop them going back to austerity."

Living conditions in Perama have deteriorated so sharply in the last few years that the area is dubbed "Ground Zero" by many of the shipyard workers. Most live in homes they built from breeze blocks with neither heating nor electricity. More than three-quarters are jobless or underemployed, almost half survive on food hand-outs from community-run soup kitchens, and almost none have access to hospital care. Health services are provided by volunteer doctors.

The collapse of Greek health provision under austerity has been devastating. An work related insurance system, the rise in unemployment and deep cuts to health budgets has left millions of Greeks without cover. Hospitals are trying to cope with zero budgets for drugs and equipment, while nurses have to care for up to 40 patients each. Vaccination programmes have almost halted and HIV infection has risen up to 200%.

Last year a study for the respected British medical journal, the Lancet, discovered government hospital spending collapsed by 26% between 2009 and 2011, and what was left was slashed by more than half between 2010 and 2014 to just 2 billion euros. Pregnant mothers have been left without any medical care, there has been a 43% rise in infant mortality, a 21% rise in stillbirths, sharp increases in rates of tuberculosis and clinical depression.

For 32 year-old Maria Gianopoulos the new Syriza government is a lifeline. A leading member of a national lobby group for sufferers of the crippling condition myasthenia gravis, the Hellenic Myasthenia Gravis Association, she said the new government is must transform Greek health care.

A former court clerk who was made redundant under the government cuts, Gianopoulos explained prohibitive charges for prescriptions and attending hospitals have been introduced since 2010. Last year the government tightened its rules so that at a stroke thousands of disabled Greeks found themselves stripped of essential benefits. Disabled protesters were met with police violence.

"One member of our society had to pay more than 200 euros for his medicine and there have been even more extreme cases. Some patients have to pay as much as 500 euros for their medicine. I regularly had to pay 40 or 50 euros a month for prescriptions and 25 euros when I attend hospital for treatment. The last year was the worst. For me it was the worst in my whole life."

She added: "When we protested in Syntagma Square against the old government the police pushed us back. With Syriza we demand that things improve. They've promised to reduce the costs of medicine and restore health budgets. That's what has been promised to the Greek people and they must deliver. It doesn't matter how tough it is for them to deliver, they must stand strong. And we'll be back in Syntagma Square to make sure they do."

22nd February 2015

The Assassination of Greece

02.20.2015 :: Analysis

Introduction: The Greek government is currently locked in a life and death struggle with the elite which dominate the banks and political decision-making centers of the European Union. What are at stake are the livelihoods of 11 million Greek workers, employees and small business people and the viability of the European Union.

If the ruling Syriza government capitulates to the demands of the EU bankers and agrees to continue the austerity programs, Greece will be condemned to decades of regression, destitution and colonial rule. If Greece decides to resist, and is forced to exit the EU, it will need to repudiate its 270 billion Euro foreign debts, sending the international financial markets crashing and causing the EU to collapse.

The leadership of the EU is counting on Syriza leaders abandoning their commitments to the Greek electorate, which as of early February 2015, is overwhelmingly (over 70%) in favor of ending austerity and debt payments and moving forward toward state investment in national economic and social development (Financial Times 7-8/2/15, p. 3). The choices are stark; the consequences have world-historical significance. The issues go far beyond local or even regional, time-bound, impacts. The entire global financial system will be affected (FT 10/2/15, p. 2).

The default will ripple to all creditors and debtors, far beyond Europe; investor confidence in the entire western financial empire will be shaken. First and foremost all western banks have direct and indirect ties to the Greek banks (FT 2/6/15, p. 3). When the latter collapse, they will be profoundly affected beyond what their governments can sustain. Massive state intervention will be the order of the day. The Greek government will have no choice but to take over the entire financial system . . . the domino effect will first and foremost effect Southern Europe and spread to the 'dominant regions' in the North and then across to England and North America (FT 9/2/15, p. 2).

To understand the origins of this crises and alternatives facing Greece and the EU, it is necessary to briefly survey the political and economic developments of the past three decades. We will proceed by examining Greek and EU relations between 1980 - 2000 and then proceed to the current collapse and EU intervention in the Greek economy. In the final section we will discuss the rise and election of Syriza, and its growing submissiveness in the context of EU dominance, and intransigence, highlighting the need for a radical break with the past relationship of 'lord and vassal'.

Ancient History: The Making of the European Empire

In 1980 Greece was admitted to the European Economic Council as a vassal state of the emerging Franco-German Empire. With the election of Andreas Papandreou, leader of the Pan-Hellenic Socialist Party, with an absolute majority in Parliament, hope arose that radical changes in domestic and foreign policy would ensue.1/ In particular, during the election campaign, Papandreou promised a break with NATO and the EEC, the revoking of the US military base agreement and an economy based on 'social ownership' of the means of production. After being elected, Papandreou immediately assured the EEC and Washington that his regime would remain within the EEC and NATO, and renewed the US military base agreement. Studies in the early 1980's commissioned by the government which documented the medium and long-term adverse results of Greece remaining in the EEU, especially the loss of control of trade, budgets and markets, were ignored by Papandreou who chose to sacrifice political independence and economic autonomy in favor of large scale transfers of funds, loans and credit from the EEC. Papandreou spoke from the balcony to the masses of independence and social justice while retaining ties to the European bankers and Greek shipping and banking oligarchs. The European elite in Brussels and Greek oligarchs in Athens retained a stranglehold on the commanding heights of the Greek political and economic system.

Papandreou retained the clientelistic political practices put in place by the previous right-wing regimes - only replacing the rightist functionaries with PASOK party loyalists.

The EEC brushed off Papandreou' phony radical rhetoric and focused on the the fact they were buying control and subservience of the Greek state by financing a corrupt, clientelistic regime which was deflecting funds for development projects to upgrade Greek economic competitiveness into building a patronage machine based on increased consumption.

The EEC elite ultimately knew that its financial stranglehold over the economy would enable it to dictate Greek policy and keep it within the boundaries of the emerging European empire.

Papandreou's demagogic "third world" rhetoric notwithstanding, Greece was deeply ensconced in the EU and NATO. Between 1981-85, Papandreou discarded his socialist rhetoric in favor of increased social spending for welfare reforms, raising wages, pensions and health coverage, while refinancing bankrupt economic firms run into the ground by kleptocratic capitalists. As a result while living standards rose, Greece's economic structure still resembled a vassal state heavily dependent on EEC finance, European tourists and a rentier economy based on real estate, finance and tourism.

Papandreou solidified Greece's role as a vassal outpost of NATO; a military platform for US military intervention in the Middle East and the eastern Mediterranean; and market for German and northern European manufactured goods.

From October 1981 to July 1989 Greek consumption rose while productivity stagnated; Papandreou won elections in

1985 using EEC funds. Meanwhile Greek debt to Europe took off ... EEC leaders chastised the misallocation of funds by Papandreou's vast army of kleptocrats but not too loudly. Brussels recognized that Papandreou and PASOK were the most effective forces in muzzling the radical Greek electorate and keeping Greece under EEC tutelage and as a loyal vassal of NATO.

Lessons for Syriza: PASOK's Short-term Reforms and Strategic Vassalage

Whether in government or out, PASOK followed in the footsteps of its rightwing adversary (New Democracy) by embracing the NATO-EEC strait-jacket.

Greece continued to maintain the highest per capita military expenditure of any European NATO member. As a result, it received loans and credits to finance short-term social reforms and large scale, long-term corruption, while enlarging the party-state political apparatus.

With the ascent of the openly neoliberal Prime Minister Costas Simitis in 2002, the PASOK regime "cooked the books", fabricated government data on its budget deficit, with the aid of Wall Street investment banks, and became a member of the European Monetary Union. By adopting the euro, Simitis furthered deepened Greece's financial subordination to the non-elected European officials in Brussels, dominated by the German finance ministry and banks.

The oligarchs in Greece made room at the top for a new breed of PASOK kleptocratic elite, which skimmed millions of military purchases, committed bank frauds and engaged in massive tax evasion.

The Brussels elite allowed the Greek middle class to live their illusions of being 'prosperous Europeans' because they retained decisive leverage through loans and accumulating debts.

Large scale bank fraud involving three hundred million euros even reached ex-Prime Minister Papandreou's office.

The clientele relations within Greece were matched by the clientele relations between Brussels and Athens.

Even prior to the crash of 2008 the EU creditors, private bankers and official lenders, set the parameters of Greek politics. The global crash revealed the fragile foundations of the Greek state - and led directly to the crude, direct interventions of the European Central Bank, the International Monetary Fund and the European Commission - the infamous "Troika". The latter dictated the 'austerity' policies as a condition for the "bail-out" which devastated the economy, provoking a major depression; impoverishing over forty percent of the population, reducing incomes by 25% and resulting in 28% unemployment.

Greece: Captivity by Invitation

Greece as a political and economic captive of the EU had no political party response. Apart from the trade unions which launched thirty general strikes between 2009 - 2014, the two major parties, PASOK and New Democracy, invited the EU takeover. The degeneration of PASOK into an appendage of oligarchs and vassal collaborator of the EU emptied the 'socialist' rhetoric of any meaning. The right wing New Democracy Party reinforced and deepened the stranglehold of the EU over the Greek economy. The troika lent the Greek vassal state funds("bail-out") which was used to pay back German, French and English financial oligarchs and to buttress private Greek banks. The Greek population was 'starved' by 'austerity' policies to keep the debt payments flowing-outward and upward.

Europe: Union or Empire?

The European economic crash of 2008/09 resounded worst on its weakest links - Southern Europe and Ireland. The true nature of the European Union as a hierarchical empire, in which the powerful states - Germany and France - could openly and directly control investment, trade, monetary and financial policy was revealed. The much vaunted EU "bailout" of Greece was in fact the pretext for the imposition of deep structural changes. These included the denationalization and privatization of all strategic economic sectors; perpetual debt payments; foreign dictates of incomes and investment policy. Greece ceased to be an independent state: it was totally and absolutely colonized.

Greece's Perpetual Crises: The End of the "European Illusion"

The Greek elite and, for at least 5 years, most of the electorate, believed that the regressive ("austerity") measures adopted - the firings, the budget cuts, the privatizations etc. were short-term harsh medicine, that would soon lead to debt reduction, balanced budgets, new investments, growth and recovery. At least that is what they were told by the economic experts and leaders in Brussels.

In fact the debt increased, the downward economic spiral continued, unemployment multiplied, the depression deepened. 'Austerity' was a class based policy designed by Brussels to enrich overseas bankers and to plunder the Greek public sector.

The key to EU pillage and plunder was the loss of Greek sovereignty. The two major parties ,New Democracy and PASOK, were willing accomplices. Despite a 55% youth (16 - 30 years old) unemployment rate, the cut-off of electricity to 300,000 households and large scale out-migration (over 175,000), the EU (as was to be expected) refused to concede that the 'austerity' formula was a failure in recovering the Greek economy. The reason the EU dogmatically stuck to a 'failed policy' was because the EU benefited from the power, privilege and profits of pillage and imperial primacy.

Moreover, for the Brussels elite to acknowledge failure in Greece would likely result in the demand to recognize failure in the rest of Southern Europe and beyond, including in France Italy and other key members of the EU (Economist 1/17/15, p. 53). The ruling financial and business elites in Europe and the US prospered through the crises and depression, by imposing cuts in social budgets and wages and salaries. To concede failure in Greece, would reverberate throughout North America and Europe, calling into question their economic policies, ideology and the legitimacy of the ruling powers. The reason that all the EU regimes back the EU insistence that Greece must continue to abide by an obviously perverse and regressive 'austerity' policy and impose reactionary "structural reforms" is because these very same rulers have sacrificed the living standards of their own labor force during the economic crises (FT 2/13/15, p. 2).

The economic crises spanning 2008/9 to the present (2015), still requires harsh sacrifices to perpetuate ruling class profits and to finance state subsidies to the private banks. Every major financial institution - the European Central Bank, the European Commission and the IMF - toes the line: no dissent or deviation is allowed. Greece must accept EU dictates or face major financial reprisals. "Economic strangulation or perpetual debt peonage" is the lesson which Brussels tends to all member states of the EU. While ostensibly speaking to Greece - it is a message directed to all states, opposition movements and trade unions who call into question the dictates of the Brussels oligarchy and its Berlin overlords.

All the major media and leading economic pundits have served as megaphones for the Brussel oligarchs. The message, which is repeated countless times, by liberals, conservatives and social democrats to the victimized nations and downwardly mobile wage and salaried workers, and small businesspeople, is that they have no choice but to accept regressive measure, slashing living conditions ("reforms") if they hope for 'economic recovery' - which, of course, has not happened after five years!

Greece has become the central target of the economic elites in Europe because, the Greek people have gone from inconsequential protests to political powers. The election of Syriza on a platform of recovering sovereignty, discarding austerity and redefining its relations with creditors to favor national development has set the stage for a possible continent-wide confrontation.

The Rise of Syriza: Dubious Legacies, Mass Struggles and Radical (Broken) Promises

The growth of Syriza from an alliance of small Marxist sects into a mass electoral party is largely because of the incorporation of millions of lower middle class public employees, pensioners and small businesspeople. Many previously supported PASOK. They voted Syriza in order to recover the living conditions and job security of the earlier period of "prosperity" (2000-2007) which they achieved within the EU. Their radical rejection of PASOK and New Democracy came after 5 years of acute suffering which might have provoked a revolution in some other country. Their radicalism began with protests, marches and strikes were attempts to pressure the rightwing regimes to alter the EU's course, to end the austerity while retaining membership in the EU.

This sector of SYRIZA is 'radical' in what it opposes today and conformist with its nostalgia for the past. -the time of euro funded vacation trips to London and Paris, easy credit to purchase imported cars and foodstuffs, to 'feel modern' and 'European' and speak English!

The politics of Syriza reflects, in part, this ambiguous sector of its electorate. In contrast Syriza also secured the vote of the radical unemployed youth and workers who never were part of the consumer society and didn't identify with "Europe". Syriza has emerged as a mass electoral party in the course of less than five years and its supporters and leadership reflects a high degree of heterogeneity.

The most radical sector, ideologically, is drawn mostly from the Marxist groups which originally came together to form the party. The unemployed youth sector joined, following the anti-police riots, which resulted from the police assassination of a young activist during the early years of the crisis. The third wave is largely made up of thousands of public workers, who were fired, and retired employees who suffered big cuts in their pensions by order of the troika in 2012. The fourth wave is ex PASOK members who fled the sinking ship of a bankrupt party.

The Syriza Left is concentrated at the mass base and among local and middle level leaders of local movements. The top leaders of Syriza in power positions are academics, some from overseas. Many are recent members or are not even party members. Few have been involved in the mass struggles - and many have few ties with the rank and file militants. They are most eager to sign a "deal" selling out the impoverished Greeks

As Syriza moved toward electoral victory in 2015, it began to shed its original program of radical structural changes (socialism) and adopt measures aimed at accommodating Greek business interests. Tsipras talked about "negotiating an agreement" within the framework of the German dominated European Union. Tsipras and his Finance Minister proposed to re-negotiate the debt, the obligation to pay and 70% of the "reforms"! When an agreement was signed they totally capitulated!

For a brief time Syriza maintained a dual position of 'opposing' austerity and coming to agreement with its creditors. It's "realist" policies reflected the positions of the new academic ministers, former PASOK members and downwardly mobile middle class. Syriza's radical gestures and rhetoric reflected the pressure of the unemployed, the youth and the mass poor who stood to lose, if a deal to pay the creditors was negotiated.

EU - SYRIZA: Concessions before Struggle Led to Surrender and Defeat

The "Greek debt" is really not a debt of the Greek people. The institutional creditors and the Euro-banks knowingly lent money to high risk kleptocrats, oligarchs and bankers who siphoned most of the euros into overseas Swiss accounts, high end real estate in London and Paris, activity devoid of any capacity to generate income to pay back the debt. In other words, the debt, in large part, is illegitimate and was falsely foisted on the Greek people.

Syriza, from the beginning of 'negotiations', did not call into question the legitimacy of the debt nor identified the particular classes and enterprise who should pay it.

Secondly, while Syriza challenged "austerity" policies it did not question the Euro organizations and EU institutions who impose it.

From its beginning Syriza has accepted membership in the EU. In the name of "realism" the Syriza government accepted to pay the debt or a portion of it, as the basis of negotiation.

Structurally, Syriza has developed a highly centralized leadership in which all major decisions are taken by Alexis Tsipras. His personalistic leadership limits the influence of the radicalized rank and file. It facilitated "compromises" with the Brussels oligarchy which go contrary to the campaign promises and may lead to the perpetual dependence of Greece on EU centered policymakers and creditors.

Moreover, Tsipras has tightened party discipline in the aftermath of his election, ensuring that any dubious compromises will not lead to any public debate or extra-parliamentary revolt.

The Empire against Greece's Democratic Outcome

The EU elite have, from the moment in which Syriza received a democratic mandate, followed the typical authoritarian course of all imperial rulers. It has demanded from Syriza (1) unconditional surrender (2) the continuation of the structures, policies and practices of the previous vassal coalition party-regimes (PASOK-New Democracy) (3) that Syriza shelve all social reforms, (raising the minimum wage, increasing pension, health, education and unemployment spending (4) that SYRIZA follow the strict economic directives and oversight formulated by the "troika" (the European Commission, the European Central Bank, and the International Monetary Fund) (5) that SYRIZA retain the current primary budget surplus target of 4.5 percent of economic output in 2015-2017.

To enforce its strategy of strangulating the new government, Brussels threatened to abruptly cut off all present and future credit facilities, call in all debt payments, end access to emergency funds and refuse to back Greek bank bonds - that provide financial loans to local businesses.

Brussels presents Syriza with the fateful "choice", of committing political suicide by accepting its dictates and alienating its electoral supporters. By betraying its mandate, Syriza will confront angry mass demonstrations. Rejecting Brussels' dictates and proceeding to mobilize its mass base, Syriza could seek new sources of financing, imposing capital controls and moving toward a radical "emergency economy".

Brussel has "stone-walled" and turned a deaf ear to the early concessions which Syriza offered. Instead Brussels sees concessions as 'steps' toward complete capitulation, instead of as efforts to reach a "compromise".

Syriza has already dropped calls for large scale debt write-offs, in favor of extending the time frame for paying the debt. Syriza has agreed to continue debt payments, provided they are linked to the rate of economic growth. Syriza accepts European oversight, provided it is not conducted by the hated "troika", which has poisonous connotations for most Greeks. However, semantic changes do not change the substance of "limited sovereignty".

Syriza has already agreed to long and middle term structural dependency in order to secure time and leeway in financing its short-term popular impact programs. All that Syriza asks is minimum fiscal flexibility under supervision of the German finance minister-some "radicals"!

Syriza has temporarily suspended on-going privatization of key infrastructure (sea- ports and airport facilities) energy and telecommunication sectors. But is has not terminated them, nor revised the past privatization. But for Brussels "sell-off" of Greek lucrative strategic sectors is an essential part of its "structural reform" agenda.

Syriza's moderate proposals and its effort to operate within the EU framework established by the previous vassal regimes was rebuffed by Germany and its 27 stooges in the EU.

The EU's dogmatic affirmation of extremist, ultra neo-liberal policies, including the practice of dismantling Greece's national economy and transferring the most lucrative sectors into the hands of imperial investors, is echoed in the pages of all the major print media. The Financial Times, Wall Street Journal, New York Times, Washington Post, Le Monde are propaganda arms of EU extremism. Faced with Brussel's intransigence and confronting the 'historic choice' of capitulation or radicalization, Syriza tried persuasion of key regimes. Syriza held numerous meetings with EU ministers. Prime Minister Alexis Tsipras and Finance Minister Yanis Vardoulakis traveled to Paris, London, Brussels, Berlin and Rome seeking a "compromise" agreement. This was to no avail. The Brussels elite repeatedly insisted:

Debts would have to be paid in full and on time.

Greece should restrict spending to accumulate a 4.5% surplus that would ensure payments to creditors, investors, speculators and kleptocrats.

The EU's lack of any economic flexibility or willingness to accept even a minimum compromise is a political decision: to humble and destroy the credibility of SYRIZA as an anti-austerity government in the eyes of its domestic supporters and potential overseas imitators in Spain, Italy, Portugal and Ireland (Economist 1/17/15, p. 53).

Conclusion

The strangulation of Syriza is part and parcel of the decade long process of the EU's assassination of Greece. A savage response to a heroic attempt by an entire people, hurled into destitution, condemned to be ruled by kleptocratic conservatives and social democrats.

Empires do not surrender their colonies through reasonable arguments or by the bankruptcy of their regressive "reforms".

Brussel's attitude toward Greece is guided by the policy of "rule or ruin". "Bail out" is a euphemism for recycling financing through Greece back to Euro-controlled banks, while Greek workers and employees are saddled with greater debt and continued dominance. Brussel's "bail out" is an instrument for control by imperial institutions, whether they are called "troika" or something else.

Brussels and Germany do not want dissenting members; they may offer to make some minor concessions so that Finance Minister Vardoulakis may claim a 'partial victory' - a sham and hollow euphemism for a belly crawl

The "bail out" agreement will be described by Tsipras-Vardoulakis as 'new' and "different' from the past or as a 'temporary' retreat. The Germans may 'allow' Greece to lower its primary budget surplus from 4.5 to 3.5 percent 'next year' - but it will still reduce the funds for economic stimulus and "postpone" raises in pensions, minimum wages etc.

Privatization and other regressive reforms will not be terminated, they will be "renegotiated". The state will retain a minority "share".

Plutocrats will be asked to pay some added taxes but not the billions of taxes evaded over the past decades.

Nor will the PASOK - New Democracy kleptocratic operatives be prosecuted for pillage and theft.

Syriza's compromises demonstrate that the looney right's (the Economist, Financial Times, NY Times, etc.) characterization of Syriza as the "hard left" or the ultra-left have no basis in reality. For the Greek electorate's "hope for the future" could turn to anger in the present. Only mass pressure from below can reverse Syriza's capitulation and Finance Minister Vardoulakis unsavory compromises. Since he lacks any mass base in the party, Tsipras can easily dismiss him, for signing off on "compromise" which sacrifices the basic interests of the people.

However, if in fact, EU dogmatism and intransigence forecloses even the most favorable deals, Tsipras and Syriza, (against their desires) may be forced to exit the Euro Empire and face the challenge of carving out a new truly radical policy and economy as a free and independent country.

A successful Greek exit from the German - Brussels empire would likely lead to the break-up of the EU, as other vassal states rebel and follow the Greek example. They may renounce not only austerity but their foreign debts and eternal interest payments. The entire financial empire - the so-called global financial system could be shaken . . .

Greece could once again become the 'cradle of democracy'.

Post-Script:Thirty years ago, I was an active participant and adviser for three years (1981-84) to Prime Minister Papandreou. He, like Tsipras, began with the promise of radical changes and ended up capitulating to Brussels and NATO and embracing the oligarchs and kleptocrats in the name of "pragmatic compromises". Let us hope, that facing a mass revolt, Prime Minister Alexis Tsipras and Syriza will follow a different path. History need not repeat itself as tragedy or farce.

---

[1] The account of the Andreas Papandreou regime draws on personal experience, interviews and observations and from my co-authored article "Greek Socialism: The Patrimonial State Revisited" in James Kurth and James Petras, Mediterranean Paradoxes: the Politics and Social Structure of Southern Europe (Oxford: Berg Press 1993/ pp. 160 -224)

James Petras was Director of the Center for Mediterranean Studies in Athens (1981-1984) and adviser to Prime Minister Andreas Papandreou (1981-84). He resigned in protest over the PM expulsion of leading trade unionists from PASOK for organizing a general strike against his 'stabilization program'.

Petras is co-author of Mediterranean Paradoxes: The Politics and Social Structure of Southern Europe. His latest books include Extractive Imperialism in the Americas (with Henry Veltmeyer); and The Politics of Empire: the US, Israel and the Middle East.

Is there a way out of the crisis within EU? The case of Greece*

By TAKIS FOTOPOULOS and GALINA TICHINSKAYA

(26.02.2015)

(The following is an edited transcript of Galina Tichinskaya's interview with Takis Fotopoulos for Pravda.ru[1])

GT: Welcome to Pravda. This is Viewpoints program, with me Galina Tichinskaya. Today we are joined by Takis Fotopoulos, a political philosopher and economist, founder of Inclusive Democracy, editor of the International Journal of Inclusive Democracy. Takis, we are very glad to see you, thank you for joining us today.

TF: Thank you for having me.

The two main political tendencies on globalization

GT: So, tell us please, which political tendency has been shown in Europe by the Syriza win in Greece?

TF: In fact, to my mind, there are two basic political tendencies today — not only in Greece, but also all over Europe, and I would say, the rest of the world.

The first tendency is what we may call the globalist tendency.[2] This is the tendency that does not question in any way globalisation, or the institutions of globalisation, like the EU, but just aims to improve the existing institutions. That's why, for example, both Syriza in Greece and Podemos in Spain and Die Linke in Germany, who belong to this tendency, simply criticise the austerity policies imposed by the EU. They never raise any question of exiting from the EU, or for creating a different kind of union of the peoples in Europe and so on. This is absolutely wrong to my mind, both for political and economic reasons, a matter perhaps to be discussed later.

The other tendency is the anti-globalisation tendency, which, in fact, is a development of the historical anti-globalisation movement that emerged in the late 1990s and early 2000s, but was crushed by the violence of the state, as well as by the systematic effort of the globalist Left that developed at the time, to emasculate this movement (World Social Forum etc[3]). So, today there is no anti-globalisation movement in the sense of an antisystemic movement. [There are] just some people who criticise globalization, but not in terms of changing the whole system of globalised economy, or, what can be called, the New World Order (NWO) of neoliberal globalisation. I am talking about *neoliberal* globalization because you can show that globalization, in a capitalist market economy, can only be neoliberal, it cannot be anything else. So, just to criticise Merkel, or whoever, that they are neoliberal is ridiculous because they had to be neoliberals, as long as they have opened and liberalised their markets. That's the essence of globalisation.

Syriza: from the old memorandums to a new one

GT: As we know, last week Eurozone ministers of finance, who had their negotiations with Greece, offered to extend the financial aid program on the country's crisis recovery, that is to extend the program with the same terms for half a year. The Greek delegation decidedly rejected this offer, but, lately, Friday talks in Brussels concluded with an agreement to extend Greece's bailout funds for 4 months. So, what's next?

TF: In fact, the EU institutions, that is, the European Commission and the European Central Bank, together with the IMF, which constituted the old Troika (as we used to call it), are again there (in Brussels and in Athens) and impose the policies that had to be implemented by Syriza, and Syriza accepted it. That's what happened last week, that is, Syriza signed a list of structural reforms, a program of structural reforms, which, in fact, is a copy of the previous Memorandum. In other words, the bailout conditions, which were imposed since 2010 —with the first Memorandum— and then in 2012, with the second Memorandum, effectively, remain in place, as something like over 70% of the conditions imposed today on Greece come from the previous Memorandum. This is something that Syriza officially denies of course, but it can be shown, and even Varoufakis, the finance minister accepted it, that 70% of the existing structural reforms in the (new) program agreed on February 20rd(and reaffirmed at the meeting of EU summit meeting on March 20th) come from the old Memorandum.

Then, there followed a conflict within the governing party. They had yesterday a series of meetings involving the parliamentary group and other party organs, and there was a clear discrepancy of views, some call it even a split, within the party: the split was mainly between one minority tendency which supports the exit from Euro ("Grexit"), and another tendency, which is the dominant tendency supported by Tsipras, the leader, Varoufakis and other leading members, which is in favour of staying both within the EU and within the Eurozone. Therefore, the government had no choice but to capitulate to everything that was imposed on them by the main organs of the Troika —which, by the way, again, for communication reasons, had its name changed from "Troika" to "the institutions"— a communication game to pass the line easier to the people.

Why there is no way out of the crisis within the EU

So, I think at the moment there is no chance of Greece leaving the Euro, unless of course the Troika itself decides it. That is, unless for some reason they decide that "we don't need Greece, it's trouble, both economic and political, so let's throw it out". But, if this does not happen, then I don't think that the present leading clique of Syriza would ever raise a question of even getting out of the Eurozone, let alone the EU —although, in fact, getting out of the Eurozone is not a solution, if it is not completed by exit from the EU and accompanied by the introduction of a policy of self-reliance (which is different from self-sufficiency).

However, there are strong economic as well as political reasons why a country like Greece cannot really get out of the crisis, as long as it remains an EU member.

The economic reasons refer to the fact that a country like Greece (or perhaps Spain and so on), cannot actually develop such a productive base, so that it could compete within a union of countries like the Eurozone. The EU, as well as the Eurozone, consist of very unequal countries in terms of economic development, in terms of productivities, and therefore in terms of competitiveness. But, either you use Marxist theory or orthodox economic theory, you can show that if you have an economic union where there are such big inequalities between members, then automatic mechanisms will be set in motion to transfer the economic surplus from the weaker members of the union to the stronger ones. So, it's not just that Germany is bad, etc. It's that Germany is the strongest economy, and therefore most of the economic surplus from the peripheral countries moves to Germany. This means that we cannot use the same policies to fight different problems. If, for example, Germany introduces austerity policies, as it did 10 years ago, the reason was that the currency was over-valued and therefore they had to reduce, to squeeze down, prices and wages in Germany. But, if you apply the same policy to a country like Greece, which is already in recession (as it was at the beginning of the crisis in 2010) the result would be further recession. And that's why in Greece, in the last 4-5 years, we had a fall in the national income by almost 1/3 and an unemployment increase to 25% of the working force, while youth unemployment is now over 50%, which is ridiculous. That is, you cannot have a functional society with these sorts of figures —

they will lead to a political and social explosion at some point. So, that's why on economic grounds it is wrong to try just to implement austerity policies, irrespective of what is the cause of low competitiveness, particularly if the cause refers to historical development, rather than to temporary fluctuations in prices and wages.

But then there are also political reasons why there is no chance of Syriza in Greece and Podemos in Spain changing the policies of the EU. There is a solid block of parties in the EU consisting of the ex-social democratic parties (which have now turned into social-liberal parties, like the Labor Party in Britain, the German Social Democratic Party, PASOK in Greece etc.) and of the conservative parties, which, together with the new members from Eastern Europe, that is the ex-Soviet bloc countries (which are fanatical anti-Russian and pro-West), will never accept any kind of changes in the EU, like the ones proposed by Tsipras in Greece and Iglesias in Spain. As recent research has shown, the common element of all these parties is that they are all convinced supporters of closer European integration, and combined they command an almost two-thirds majority in the European Parliament, with 478 out of the 751 seats.[4]

So, that's why there is no way out of the crisis *within* the EU, because, on both political and economic grounds, continuation of EU membership would mean the same sort of policies that we have now. It does not matter how you present or package it, the result will be the same thing.

Why Keynesian policies are impossible for any EU member state

GT: One of the key figures of the Greek government, Yanis Varoufakis, the finance minister, who graduated from the University of Essex calls himself an erratic Marxist. Why?

TF: Actually, Varoufakis' theory and praxis have no relation at all to either Marxist theory or libertarian theory —at least left libertarian theory— (he calls himself also "libertarian Marxist"), as one could easily conclude from his self-presentation in the *Guardian*.[5] In fact, he is just a liberal Keynesian, or rather a pseudo-Keynesian because to implement Keynesian policies you need a nation-state, you need sovereignty, and the main characteristic of the EU is that all members, particularly all members taking part in the Eurozone, in fact, sign away their own economic and therefore national sovereignty the moment they join it. They are not any more nation-states in the sense that we used to know in the past, as they do not control their economic policies at all. Thus, monetary policies are directly controlled by the European Central Bank, not by the central bank of each member country. Then, fiscal policies are also controlled by the same elites at the centre of the EU, albeit indirectly, through various conditions they impose on members in order to improve competitiveness (balanced budgets etc.). For example, in Greece they have imposed, through the last memorandum, the requirement that there should be a surplus in the budget of 4 to 4.5% of the GDP, and Varoufakis has celebrated that he managed to persuade the "institutions" to have this requirement reduced to 2% or less, although this is something that has not yet been decided. However, even

2%, in fact, is too much, particularly for countries in the EU periphery. Governments should be able to spend money, particularly in a country like Greece, in order to use it for public investment and expand the production capacity, through changing the production structure and correspondingly the consumption structure. It's only by changing the production and consumption structures of a country, particularly in the EU periphery, that you can achieve some sort of competitiveness in order to compete in this open market. And of course you cannot rely on private investment to achieve such a radical restructuring of the production structure, as the EU stipulates! So, in effect, peripheral EU members are forcibly locked in a vicious circle: they have to improve competitiveness to survive cut-throat competition, but as they have to rely mainly on foreign investment to restructure production, if this is not forthcoming, they have to squeeze wages to improve competitiveness "artificially", through austerity policies — i.e. further recession!

National vs. Transnational sovereignty

But if a government does not control its economic policy, then it does not have any economic sovereignty. And if you do not have any economic sovereignty, you don't have national sovereignty. In fact, therefore, these countries, the EU peripheral countries, do not have any economic sovereignty, and therefore any national sovereignty. What happens is that the advanced capitalist countries in the North, like Germany, France, Britain (although Britain is not a member of Eurozone it's still a member of the EU), have a different sort of sovereignty, what I call *transnational sovereignty*, in the sense that lots of the transnational corporations are based in these countries, and it can be shown that they control the world economy today.[6] Consequently, transnational corporations possess also a very significant degree of political power, and in fact it had been shown in the past that the European Round Table of Industrialists, which is an informal meeting of the main transnational corporations in Europe, had drafted all the main constitutional treaties that the EU implements now.[7] That is, the Maastricht treaty, the Lisbon treaty and so on. And the sort of constitution these treaties imposed was the essence of neoliberalism. In other words, all the neoliberal measures that are implemented today by the EU are the neoliberal policies suggested by the transnational corporations.

So, today we have a system of double, I would say, sovereignty. We have first transnational sovereignty, which means that some countries, the advanced capitalist countries (mainly the G7 countries), from where most of the transnational corporations originate, have a very significant degree of transnational economic power, and not only. They also have transnational political/ cultural/ propaganda power, and so on. That's how they control the world through what I called, the transnational elite, which is simply the elites based in these countries. These are the elites, which control the world today. That is, although there is no formal body expressing them, still, by controlling the various world institutions, the economic institutions (the IMF, the World Bank, the European Central Bank and so on), or political institutions (like the UN and so on, apart from NATO, etc.), they control, in fact, the world, because they control all forms of power. This is a transnational kind of power; it's not national sovereignty. It's transnational sovereignty, in the sense that it relies on controlling political, economic and other forms of power at the transnational, rather than the national, level.

So the only way for a country today to have any sort of national power, or national sovereignty, is if it breaks from the NWO of neoliberal globalisation. And that's why I think that the Eurasian Union could be a step is this direction. If it develops, as a union of sovereign nations (that is, of nations that maintain their national sovereignty), into both a political and an economic union. Then, it could perfectly be an alternative pole to the present unipolar world. Because there is no doubt that, at the moment, we have a unipolar world, as it is shown by the fact that all forms of transnational power today are mainly controlled by the Transnational Elite. But, If the Eurasian Union develops and flourishes, and countries like Greece, as well as other countries in Latin America and so on, join it, then, this would create another pole. Then we could have a real bipolar world, which is in fact the only way you can challenge the present NWO. That is, through an economic and political union like this, in which countries maintain their national sovereignty and their economic sovereignty, so that they could also have different principles to base their co-operation, instead of being involved in a cut-throat competition, as is the fundamental principle imposed by the NWO.

The role of BRICS in the NWO and the myth of the present multi-polar world

GT: Could Greece ask aid from the BRICS Development Bank?

TF: The BRICS countries, apart from Russia, which does have a significant degree of national and economic sovereignty, do not have any significant transnational sovereignty and at the same time, being fully integrated into the NWO, do not have any significant national sovereignty either. On the other hand, Russia although itself integrated at the moment into the NWO through the World Trade Organization, and so on, still, compared to all other BRICS countries, has the highest degree of both national and economic sovereignty. That's why it's very important, if Russia helps the movement for the Eurasian Union to become a real political and economic union of sovereign nations, rather than just a free trade zone, as globalists in the West and Russia itself want. The other countries in BRICS, like China and India, are much more integrated into the NWO, in the sense that both the Chinese and the Indian economic "miracles" are based on the massive influx of transnational corporations to exploit the very low production cost there. So, BRICS potentially may be helpful in this process of creating an alternative pole, provided, however, that they start breaking the close ties they have at the moment with the NWO and the Transnational Elite. Otherwise, if they try to play it safe, as for example India does at the moment, and to some extent China, as when they try to have good relations both with the Transnational Elite (US, EU) and also with Russia, then obviously they are irrelevant to the process of creating a real alternative pole to the NWO.

With regard to the question you asked whether Greece should ask the BRICS' help, assuming of course their present integration into the NWO, then of course, trade and investment relations with these countries might help — instead of leaving such relations being controlled mainly by the EU, as at present. But we should not forget that Greece might not be even able to expand freely these sorts of links with BRICS, as long as it remains a member of the EU. That is, as long as Greece is in the EU, then the EU could boycott any kind of expanded relations with the BRICS countries. It happened before with the Burgas-Alexandroupolis oil pipeline,when President Putin signed an agreement with the Greek government (Karamanlis at the time), and then the EU boycotted this agreement in every way possible (eventually even by taking action leading to the replacement of Karamanlis with a much more obedient organ to the NWO, i.e. George Papandreou), and finally achieved the cancellation of an agreement which was important for Greece (from the economic and geopolitical viewpoints). So, it's not just a matter of whether it would be good for Greece to expand economic relations with BRICS. Everything depends on what sort of Greece we are talking about. The present Greece, which is a member of both the EU and the Eurozone, (or even if it was just an EU member) cannot significantly expand its links with BRICS or Russia, unless the EU approves it.

The sanctions against Russia and Greece

GT: In case of leaving the Eurozone, will Greece support the hostile EU policy towards Russia?

TF: Again, let's see what happened in the last meeting of the EU foreign ministers in Brussels, ten days ago. Syriza, before it was elected, was against the sanctions, and the present foreign minister has written repeatedly against economic sanctions on Russia. However, when they became government, both this foreign minister and the Syriza government changed route. That is, what they did in the Brussels meeting was just to approve the sanctions and simply try to reduce the duration period of these sanctions from a year to six months. But of course this meant that, implicitly, he accepted the sanctions in principle. In fact, when the same foreign minister went to Kiev last week, he said "yes, the sanctions are not always bad, it depends on what sort of sanctions we talk about and why". It is therefore clear that as long as Greece remains a member of the EU and the Eurozone, then it would have to dance to the orchestra's tune and the orchestra is conducted not by Greece, but by the elites in the EU, in other worlds, Germany and the other main countries within the EU. So they would have to follow the policies imposed by them on any major foreign policy issue like Russia, Ukraine, and support any kind of war they may launch in the Middle East in the near future, and so on. Of course, if Greece moved out of the EU (not just the Eurozone), then things would be different. Then everything would be open. That is, then, you may expect that Greece would follow a very different policy because the Greek people, as you know, are very close to the Russian people, for historical and cultural reasons, and they would surely want to have these sanctions abolished on reasons of principle, This, quite apart from the issue of economic damage that Greek farmers have suffered for no reason at all, just because some elites decided to impose sanctions on Russia and, as a result, now Greek farmers cannot sell much of their produce.

GT: Takis, thank you very much for joining us today and taking the time.

TF: Thank you for having me; it was a pleasure to meet you.

GT: Thank you. And this was Viewpoints program with me, Galina Tichinskaya. Thank you for watching us.

Takis Fotopoulos is a political philosopher, editor of Society & Nature/ Democracy and Nature/The International Journal of Inclusive Democracy. He has also been a columnist for the Athens Daily Eleftherotypia since 1990. Between 1969 and 1989 he was Senior Lecturer in Economics at the University of North London (formerly Polytechnic of North London). He is the author of over 25 books and over 1,000 articles, many of which have been translated into various languages.

Syriza Foreign Minister Kotzias dancing and singing with NATO war chiefs

Greece and the EU: First as Tragedy, Second as Farce, Third as Vassal State

First, the denial came as tragedy: When the Greek majority elected Syriza to government and their debts increased, the economy plunged further into depression and unemployment and poverty soared. The Greek people voted for Syriza believing its promises of 'a new course'. Immediately following their victory, Syriza reneged on their promise to restore sovereignty – and end the subjugation of the Greek people to the economic dictates of overseas bankers, bureaucrats and political oligarchs. Instead Syriza kept Greece in the oligarchical imperialist bloc, portraying the European Union as an association of independent sovereign countries. What began as a great victory of the Greek people turned into a tragic strategic retreat. >From their first day in office, Syriza led the Greek people down the blind alley of total submission to the German empire.

Then the tragedy turned into farce when the Greek people refused to acknowledge the impending betrayal by their elected leaders. They were stunned, but mute, as Syriza emptied the Greek treasury and offered even greater concessions, including acceptance of the illegal and odious debts incurred by private bankers, speculators and political kleptocrats in previous regimes.

True to their own vocation as imperial overlords, the EU bosses saw the gross servility of Syriza as an invitation to demand more concessions – total surrender to perpetual debt peonage and mass impoverishment. Syriza's demagogic leaders, Yanis Varoufakis and Alexis Tsipras, shifting from fits of hysteria to infantile egotism, denounced 'the Germans and their blackmail' and then performed a coy belly-crawl at the feet of the 'Troika', peddling their capitulation to the bankers as 'negotiations' and referring to their overlords as . . . 'partners'.

Syriza, in office for only 5 months brought Greece to the edge of total bankruptcy and surrender, then launched the 'mother of all deceptions' on the Greek people: Tsipras convoked a 'referendum' on whether Greece should reject or accept further dictates and cuts to bare bones destitution. Over 60% of the Greek people voted a resounding NO to further plunder and poverty.

In Orwellian fashion, the megalomaniac Tsipras immediately re-interpreted the 'NO' vote as a mandate to capitulation to the imperial powers, accepting the EU bankers' direct supervision of the regime's implementation of Troika's policies – including drastic reductions of Greek pensions, doubling the regressive 'VAT' consumption tax on vital necessities and a speed-up of evictions of storeowners and householders behind in their mortgage payments. Thus Greece became a vassal state: Nineteenth century colonialism was re-imposed in the 21st century.

Colonialism by Invitation

Greek politicians, whether Conservative or Socialist, have openly sought to join the German-led imperial bloc known as the European Union, even when it was obvious that the Greek economy and financial system was vulnerable to domination by the powerful German ruling class.

From the beginning, the Greek Panhellenic Socialist Party (PASOK) and their Conservative counterparts refused to recognize the class basis of the European Union. Both political factions and the Greek economic elites, that is, the kleptocrats who governed and the oligarchs who ruled, viewed entry into the EU as an opportunity for taking and faking loans, borrowing, defaulting and passing their enormous debts on to the public treasury!

Widely circulating notions among the Left that 'Germany is responsible' for the Greek crisis are only half true, while the accusations among rightwing financial scribes that the 'Greek people are spendthrifts' who brought on their own crisis is equally one-sided. The reality is more complex:

The crash and collapse of the Greek economy was a product of an entrenched parasitic rentier ruling class – both Socialist and Conservative – which thrived on borrowing at high interest rates and speculating in non-productive economic activities while imposing an astronomical military budget. They engaged in fraudulent overseas financial transactions while grossly manipulating and fabricating financial data to cover-up Greece's unsustainable trade and budget deficits.

German and other EU exporters had penetrated and dominated the Greek markets. The bankers charged exorbitant interest rates while investors exploited cheap Greek labor. The creditors ignored the obvious risks because Greek rulers were their willing accomplices in the ongoing pillage.

Clearly entry into and continued membership in the EU has largely benefited two groups of elites: the German rulers and the Greek rentiers: The latter received short-term financial grants and transfers while the former gained powerful levers over the banks, markets and, most important, established cultural-ideological hegemony over the Greek political class. The Greek elite and middle class believed 'they were Europeans' – that the EU was a beneficent arrangement and a source of prosperity and upward mobility. In reality, Greek leaders were merely accomplices to the German conquest of Greece. And the major part of the middle class aped the views of the Greek elite.

The financial crash of 2008-2009 ended the illusions for some but not most Greeks. After 6 years of pain and suffering a new version of the old political class came to power: Syriza! Syriza brought in new faces and rhetoric but operated with the same blind commitment to the EU. The Syriza leadership believed they were "partners".

The road to vassalage is rooted deep in the psyche of the political class. Instead of recognizing their subordinate membership in the EU as the root cause of their crisis, they blamed 'the Germans, the bankers, Angela Merkel, Wolfgang Schnauble , the IMF, the Troika… The Greek rulers and middle class were in fact both victims and accomplices.

The German imperial regime loaned money from the tax revenues of German workers to enable their complicit Greek vassals to pay back the German bankers… German workers complained. The German media deflected criticism by blaming the 'lazy Greek cheats'. Meanwhile, the Greek oligarch-controlled media deflected criticism of the role of the parasitical political class back to the 'Germans'. This all served to obscure the class dynamics of empire building — colonialism by invitation. The ideology of blaming peoples, instead of classes, is pitting German workers against Greek employees and pensioners. The German masses support their bankers, while the Greek masses have elected and followed Syriza – their traitors.

From Andreas Papandreou to Alexis Tsipras: Misconceptions about the European Union

After Syriza was elected a small army of instant experts, mostly leftist academics from Canada, the US and Europe, sprang up to write and speak, usually with more heat than light, on current Greek political and economic developments. Most have little knowledge or experience of Greek politics, particularly its history and relations with the EU over the past thirty five years.

The most important policy decisions shaping the current Syriza government's betrayal of Greek sovereignty go back to the early 1980's when I was working as an adviser to PASOK Prime Minister Andreas Papandreou. At that time, I was party to an internal debate of whether to continue within the EU or leave. Papandreou was elected on an anti EU, anti NATO platform, which, like Tsipras, he promptly reneged on– arguing that 'there were no alternatives'. Even then, there were international and Greek academic sycophants, as there are today, who argued that membership in the EU was the only realistic alternative- it was the 'only possibility'. The 'possibilistas" at that time, operating either from ignorance or deceit, were full of bluster and presumption. They denied the underlying power realities in the structure of the EU and dismissed the class capacity of the working and popular masses to forge an alternative. Then, as now, it was possible to develop independent alternative relations with Europe, Russia, China, the Middle East and North Africa. The advantages of maintaining a protected market, a robust tourist sector and an independent monetary system were evident and did not require EU membership (or vassalage).

Above all, what stood out in both leaders, Andreas Papandreou and Alexis Tsipras, was their profound misconception of the class nature of the dominant forces in the EU. In the 1980's Germany was just beginning to recover its imperial reach. By the time Syriza-Tsipras rose to power (January 2015), Germany's imperial power was undeniable. Tsipras' misunderstanding of this reality can be attributed to his and his 'comrades' rejection of class and imperial analyses. Even academic Marxists, who spouted Marxist theory, never applied their abstract critiques of capitalism and imperialism to the concrete realities of German empire building and Greece's quasi-colonial position within the EU. They viewed their role as that of 'colonial reformers' –imagining that they were clever enough to 'negotiate' better terms in the German-centered EU. They inevitably failed because Berlin had a built-in majority among its fervently neo-liberal ex-communist satellites plus the IMF, French and English imperial partners. Syriza was no match for this power configuration. Then there was the bizarre delusion among the Syriza intellectuals that European capitalism was more benign than the US version.

EU membership has created scaffolding for German empire-building. The take off point was West Germany's annexation of East Germany. This was soon followed by the incorporation of the rightwing regimes in the Baltic and Balkans as subordinate members of the EU – their public assets were snapped up by Germany corporations at bargain prices. The third step was the systematic break-up of Yugoslavia and the incorporation of Slovenia into the German orbit. The fourth step was the takeover of key sectors of the Polish and Czech economies and the exploitation of cheap skilled labor from Bulgaria, Romania, Hungary and other satellite states.

Without firing a shot, German empire-building has revolved around making loans and financial transfers to the new subordinate member states in the EU. These financial transactions were predicated upon the following conditions: 1) Privatization and sale of the new member states' prized public assets to mainly German as well as other EU investors and 2) Forcing member states to dismantle their social programs, approve massive lay-offs and meet impossible fiscal targets. In other words, expansion of the contemporary German empire required austerity measures, which transformed the ex-communist countries into satellites, vassals and sources of mercenaries – a pattern which is now playing out in Greece.

The reason these new German 'colonies' (especially Poland and the Baltic States) insist on the EU imposing harsh austerity measures on Greece, is that they went through the same brutal process convincing their own beleaguered citizens that there was no alternative –

resistance was futile. Any successful demonstration by Greek workers, farmers and employees that resistance to empire was possible would expose the corrupt relationship between these client leaders and the German imperial order. In order to preserve the foundations of the new imperial order, Germany has had to take a hardline on Greece. Otherwise the recently incorporated colonial subjects in the Baltic, Balkan and Central Europe states might "re-think" the brutal terms of their own incorporation to the European Union. This explains the openly punitive approach to Greece – turning it into the 'Haiti of Europe' analogous to the US' long standing brutalization of the rebellious Haitians – as an object lesson to its own Caribbean and Latin American clients.

The root cause of German intransigence has nothing to do with the political personalities or quirks of Angela Merkle and Wolfgang Schnauble: Such imperial leaders do not operate out of neurotic vindictiveness. Their demand for total Greek submission is an imperative of German empire-building, a continuation of the step-by-step conquest of Europe.

German empire-building emphasizes economic conquests, which go hand-in-hand with US empire-building based on military conquests. The same economic satellites of Germany also serve as sites for US military bases and exercises encircling Russia; these vassal states provide mercenary soldiers for US imperial wars in South Asia, Iraq, Syria and elsewhere.

Syriza's economic surrender is matched by its spineless sell-out to NATO, its support of sanctions against Russia and its embrace of US policies toward Syria, Lebanon and Israel.

Germany and its imperial partners have launched a savage attack on the working people of Greece, usurping Greek sovereignty and planning to seize 50 billion Euros of vital Greek public enterprises, land and resources. This alone should dispels the myth, promoted especially by the French social democratic demagogue Jacques Delores, that European capitalism is a benign form of 'social welfarism' and an 'alternative' to the savage Anglo-American version capitalism.

What has been crucial to previous and current versions of empire-building is the role of a political collaborator class facilitating the transition to colonialism. Here is where social democrats, like Alexis Tsipras, who excel in the art of talking left while embracing the right, flatter and deceive the masses into deepening austerity and pillage.

Instead of identifying the class enemies within the EU and organizing an alternative working class program, Tsipras and his fellow collaborators pose as EU 'partners', fostering class collaboration – better to serve imperial Europe: When the German capitalists demanded their interest payments, Tsipras bled the Greek economy. When German capitalists sought to dominate Greek markets, Tsipras and Syriza opened the door by keeping Greece in the EU. When German capital wanted to supervise the take-over of Greek properties, Tsipras and Syriza embraced the sell-off.

There is clear class collaboration within the Greek elite in the destruction of nation's sovereignty: Greek banker oligarchs and sectors of the commercial and tourist elite have acted as intermediaries of the German empire builders and they personally benefit from the German and EU takeover despite the destitution of the Greek public.

Such economic intermediaries, representing 25% of the electorate, have become the main political supporters of the Syriza-Tsipras betrayal. They join with the EU elite applauding Tsipras' purge of left critics and his authoritarian seizure of legislative and executive power! This collaborator class will never suffer from pension cuts, layoffs and unemployment. They will never have to line up at crippled banks for a humiliating dole of 65 Euros of pension money. These collaborators have hundreds of thousands and millions stashed in overseas bank accounts and invested in overseas real estate. Unlike the Greek masses, they are 'European' first and foremost – willing accomplices of German empire builders!

Tragic Beginnings: The Greek People Elect a Trojan Horse

Syriza is deeply rooted in Greek political culture .A leadership of educated mascots serving overseas European empire-builders. Syriza is supported by academic leftists who are remote from the struggles, sacrifices and suffering of the Greek masses. Syriza's leadership emerged on the scene as ideological mentors and saviors with heady ideas and shaky hands. They joined forces with downwardly mobile middle class radicals who aspired to rise again via the traditional method: radical rhetoric, election to office, negotiations and transactions with the local and foreign elite and betrayal of their voters. Theirs is a familiar

political road to power, privilege and prestige. In this regard, Tsipras personifies an entire generation of upwardly mobile opportunists, willing and able to sellout

Greece and its people. He perpetuates the worst political traditions: In campaigns he promoted consumerism over class consciousness (discarding any mobilization of the masses upon election!). He is a useful fool, embedded in a culture of clientelism, kleptocracy, tax evasion, predatory lenders and spenders – the very reason his German overlords tolerated him and Syriza, although on a short leash!

Tsipras' Syriza has absolute contempt for democracy. He embraces the 'Caudillo Principle': one man, one leader, one policy! Any dissenters invite dismissal!

Syriza has utterly submitted to imperial institutions, the Troika and their dictates, NATO and above all the EU, the Eurozone. Tsipras/ Syriza reject outright independence and freedom from imperial dictates. In his 'capitulation to the Germans' Tsipra engaged in histrionic theatrics, but by his own personal dictate, the massive 'NO to EU' vote was transformed into a YES.

The cruelest political crime of all has been Tsipras running down the Greek economy, bleeding the banks, emptying the pension funds and freezing everyday salaries while 'blaming the bankers', in order to force the mass of Greeks to accept the savage dictates of his imperial overlords or face utter destitution!

The Ultimate Surrender

Tsipras and his sycophants in Syriza, while constantly decrying Greece's subordination to the EU empire-builders and claiming victimhood, managed to undermine the Greek people's national consciousness in less than 6 months. What had been a victorious referendum and expression of rejection by three-fifths of the Greek voters turned into a prelude to a farcical surrender by empire collaborators. The people's victory in the referendum was twisted to represent popular support for a Caudillo. While pretending to consult the Greek electorate, Tsipras manipulated the popular will into a mandate for his regime to push Greece beyond debt peonage and into colonial vassalage.

Tsipras is a supreme representation of Adorno's authoritarian personality: On his knees to those above him, while at the throat of those below.

Once he has completed his task of dividing, demoralizing and impoverishing the Greek majority, the local and overseas ruling elites will discard him like a used condom, and he will pass into history as a virtuoso in deceiving and betraying the Greek people.

Epilogue:

Syriza's embrace of hard-right foreign policies should not be seen as the 'result of outside pressure', as its phony left supporters have argued, but rather a deliberate choice. So

far, the best example of the Syriza regime's reactionary policies is its signing of a military agreement with Israel.

According to the Jerusalem Post (July 19, 2015), the Greek Defense Minister signed a mutual defense and training agreement with Israel, which included joint military exercises. Syriza has even backed Israel's belligerent position against the Islamic Republic of Iran, endorsing Tel Aviv's ridiculous claim that Teheran represents a terrorist threat in the Middle East and Mediterranean. Syriza and Israel have inked a mutual military support pact that exceeds any other EU member agreement with Israel and is only matched in belligerence by Washington's special arrangements with the Zionist regime.

Israel's ultra-militarist 'Defense' Minister Moshe Yaalon, (the Butcher of Gaza), hailed the agreement and thanked the Syriza regime for 'its support'. It is more than likely that Syriza's support for the Jewish state explains its popularity with Anglo-American and Canadian 'left' Zionists…

Syriza's strategic ties with Israel are not the result of EU 'pressure' or the dictates of the 'Troika'. The agreement is a radical reversal of over a half-century of Greek support for the legitimate national rights of the Palestinian people

against the Israeli terrorist state. This military pact, like the Syriza regime's economic capitulation to the German ruling class, is deeply rooted in the 'colonial ideology', which permeates Tsipras' policies. He has taken Greece a significant step 'forward' from economic vassal to a mercenary client of the most retrograde regime in the Mediterranean.

The **'OXI'** Referendum: Eyewitness Reports

11th July 2015
251 votes for €13b cuts.
Syriza loses parliamentary majority down to 145 MPs
2 Syriza MPs vote openly NO
Lafazanis, Konstantopoulou, Lapavitsas, Stratoulis abstain.
So two ministers Energy and Labour are probably on way out.

If agreement is reached (not 100%) either reshuffle with new grand coalition with all the other Memorandum parties or new elections...

Either which way Syriza will go the way of LAOS, PASOK, Dimar....

5th July 2015
Massive NO vote 61% to 38% with around 40% abstention
Class based vote Perama (dockworkers) 77% NO Ekali 85% YES
No electoral region a YES vote
Around 5.5m voted
Left increased vote by around 25% from 2.7m to 3.3m since January 2015
Rightists collapsed to 2m from 2.3m
Massive media propaganda using pensioners didn't work, Greeks no longer frightened of Grexit.
Invalid/blank 5.8%
Spontaneous party in Athens, Sindagma Sq

OXI Rally

After yesterday's demo where more than 700k turned up it is clear that none of the existing political formations can impose their will on the Greek people. Unless one believes hungry stomachs can be filled. The rally in Sindagma is more important than the actual Referendum.
a) the rally was full of Greeks. There were no illegal immigrants there.
b) average working class people from daily life.
c) everywhere there were Greek flags with communist ones. Absent were all flags of the European union.

d) the size of the rally just in Athens indicates a big OXI vote in the cities. It's a class vote based on those devastated by austerity.
e) Syriza will have problems turning any OXI vote against the numbers seen at the rally.
f) Tsipras was visibly shaken by both size and passion of the rally....

3rd July 2015
Kammenos stated army will guarantee safety and security
IMF asked openly for a 33% cut in Greece's Debt
E Tsakalotos Syrizas Chief Negotiator stated we went to Referendum as we couldn't pass cuts
Last YES and NO rallies tonight
KKE rally abysmally small

2nd July 2015
Lapavitsas stating we are staying in Euros on Syriza s programme. In other words Merkels.
Banks open for pensioners, no issues today.
Adverts started pro EU campaigns.
Syriza MPs emerged openly against Referendum
Two ANEL MPs have turned
If YES vote Varoufakis stated that he will resign
Syriza blaming correctly closure of Banks on ECB

1st July 2015
State of play re Greek Referendum
Don't count your chickens before they hatch! Influence of corporate media may not be as powerful. On the ground when leafletting most people are for NO. Many believe the

whole event could be stage managed to sell a new package of cuts using the Debt (as negotiable now on the table) so Syriza can sell it internally. Its alleged Varoufakis as I give us the Debt on table we will give you the Referendum...But with $3trillion losses on stockmarkets worldwide the longer this continues the worse it becomes...Schauble said With a NO vote Greece remains in Euro....ND candidates had breakdowns on tv when they heard IMF wasnt paid. ECB could pull plug on Monday. Greece has printing presses and can print Euros to cover cash withdrawals. The issue is whether the Syriza leadership wants a resounding NO vote. Which so far it clearly doesn't.

Tsipras made new proposal a new MoU around €30b without IMF
Media stories about ECB collapsing two systemic banks to influence voters intentions.
Rightist rally 'Staying in Europe'. ND nutters on tv going mad about closed banks.
Dragasakis stated we might cancel referendum.
Zoi (House Speaker) said it can't be cancelled.
IMF default occurred.

30th June 2015
Massive NO demo in Sindagma by Syriza.
Tsipras won't pay IMF tonight so default.
Chinese stock market opens 25% down in 3 days.
Tsipras mentioned possibility of double referendum Irish style...
Syriza reps weirdly absent from corporate news networks.

29th June 2015

Banks to re open with €60 daily withdrawal limit ie €1800pcm via ATMs

Average pensions are €500pcm Minimum wage €600 Pensioners without bank cards will be able to go into Greek Ethniki bank and withdraw the whole pension in one go.

Asian European stock markets plunge.

Rally tonight 730pm by Syriza in Sundagma Sq

All public transport free until banks reopen

Local NO campaigns have started in every Athenian sq.

Junquer said we should vote YES.

ATMs working people can withdraw €60

Tourists can withdraw money with no controls.

26th June 2015

Tsipras offered EURO 8b in cuts.

Troika demanded EURO 12b.

Syriza could not remain intact nor Greek business in tourism or agriculture.

This is too little too late but better late than never.

A vote NO signals a break.

The road points only one way Grexit; Drachma; Exit EU; Cancellation of Debt.

This collision course is inevitable. Its not happening the way we want but its happening.

Pensions are paid at end of month and people on extremely tight budgets go to cashpoints early.

27th June 2015
178 voted for Referendum proposals.
KKE voted it down with PASOK, ND, Potami.
PASOK labelled proposal for Referendum a coup.

Varoufakis stated if Troika does change position and come to an agreement we will vote YES.
GD voted with Syriza. Their leaders was for Euro last Thursday in newspaper interview yesterday one of their spokespersons came out in support of Drachma.

Schauble stated we can't have both Tsipras and Greece in Euro.
Tusk stated Greces role in Euro is unquestionable.

28th June 2015
Repercussions of KKE decision to vote against Referendum hits members hard with disbelief.
Presstitutes circulate stories about ELA withdrawals fake.
Stories about imposition of capital controls by Varoufakis also fake during day.
Samaras trying to get President to not collaborate on upcoming referendum.
Bankrun by media appears to be fake just by travelling around two districts.

Cabinet meeting 8pm announcement that Stock Exchange Banks closed for one week to avoid rightist destabilization of Referendum.

2k strong demo-rally outside Sindagma Sq by Antarsya Mars against EU calling for 'Default rtn to Drachma'. Syriza brings out riot police on steps in Parliament. ND calls for Tsipras to cancel Referendum. Merkel calls for meeting of all political leaders in Germany.

Printed t shirts in Skouries Gold mine by protestor. "Welcome Tsipras Kolotoumba (Flipflopper)"

Staying in Europe?

Hands open for a bag of food. But let us not spoil the image. The issue is **'Staying in Europe'**.

***

Hundred long lines for a plate of food. What the issue as long as we are **'Staying in Europe'**.

***

Congregation of hundreds of people, conflicts, pushing and shoving for a free 'meal', humans searching for food in dustbins. The issue for all of us to **'Stay in Europe'**.

***

It would be great if this was a plastic picture for Greece. Hopefully it would be a product of the 'montage' of some type of 'antieuropean populism'

Unfortunately it is a real picture of millions of Greeks who have a different view than the 'european ideal', that which is sold by Theodorakis 'Potami' (River party)

***

This is the Greece whom naturally the locals don't stay or its foreign dynasties. It's been crushed by class interests which have been baptised as 'national ideals' from the forces of particular 'populism', ie the establishment.

This Greece where lines are formed for kilometres for a bag of tomatoes is the Greece of the stolen dignity of food kitchens and lines of homeless. Decaying Greece of the 1.5m unemployed. The Greece of homemade fires. The Greece of the thousands of young you emigrate abroad. The Greece of Ottoman style tax brigandry. The Greece of 700k that are underfed.
This is the Greece of **'Staying in Europe'**. Here there is no 'creative ambiguity'...

***

In the Greece of **'Staying in Europe'**, they who threaten us that we will become... Zambia, are the same who have ensured that we have social and labour conditions akin to ...Somalia. For instance:
Millions of people who are found under the minimum level of poverty.
One million unemployed who are working and remain unpayed for up to 12 months. Extending the income policy of disparity amongst the richest and the poorest Greeks by 7.5%. A fact that brings Greece to the first decade of countries with the biggest disparities on a global level, to be challenging first place amongst Chile, Mexico and Turkey!

Thousands of workers in the private sector who instead of being paid a wage are paid by ...coupons so they can purchase items from supermarkets.

This is the Greece with which the 'saviours' with the flag of the permanent demonstrator Georgiadi they chant 'We are **Staying in Europe'**...

***

In the Greece of 'Staying in Europe' they who deceive the electorate and their supporters they paint their 'rolex's' as ours and their Cayennes as ours are the same who have imposed Bulgarian wages.

7 out of 10 workers work for less that E1k a month.

4 out 10 workers (40%) are paid less than E630net a month.

30% of those insured in state system IKA (3 out of 10) have a monthly wage under or around the national minimum wage (E586)

25% of the labour force is paid a wage lower than that of the unskilled worker.

51% of the new labour contracts which are signed in the private sector are under the regime of part time employment, under E500 a month.

Thousands of young up till 25 year old are working for 180 Euros a month for a 4hr work at E2.25 a day.

Thousands of workers in the private sector who instead of being paid a wage are paid by ...coupons so they can purchase items from supermarkets.

This is the Greece with which the 'saviours' with the flag of the permanent demonstrator Georgiadi they chant 'We are **Staying in Europe'**...

***

In Greece of '**Staying in Europe'** the majority of the people is in a situation much worse than that of bankruptcy. Only one element can be seen: The final bills towards the banks, public sector and insurance coffers are more than the whole GDP of the country!
GB'>7 out of 10 workers work for less that E1k a month. 4 out 10 workers (40%) are paid less than E630net a month. 30% of those insured in state system IKA (3 out of 10) have a monthly wage under or around the national minimum wage (E586) 25% of the labour force is paid a wage lower than that of the unskilled worker. 51% of the new labour contracts which are signed in the private sector

are under the regime of part time employment, under E500 a month. Thousands of young up till 25 year old are working for 180 Euros a month for a 4hr work at E2.25 a day.

Thousands of workers in the private sector who instead of being paid a wage are paid by ...coupons so they can purchase items from supermarkets.

This is the Greece with which the 'saviours' with the flag of the permanent demonstrator Georgiadi they chant 'We are **Staying in Europe'**...

***

We are '**Staying in Europe'** then. But a little honesty doesn't do harm. **Staying in Europe** either in the form of

'We Belong to the West' or with the form of 'negotiations' which extends the old Memorandums and leads to '47 pages' to new MoU, is about a Europe which is called the 'European Union', is empowered by Schauble and has transformed Greece into Bulgaria (wages) transformed it into Somalia (levels of social justice) and has returned to levels of Ottoman (taxation).

***

We are **'Staying in Europe'** then. But lets us not close our eyes. In this Greece of this 'Europe' the astonishing pictures provided show this precisely what large layers of the population live like.

They are pictures which were repeated many times over in Nea Smirni, in Peristeri, in Kolonos, Drapetsona, Nikaia, Menidi Elefsina and Thessaloniki.

Pictures which show reveal other things: Their hatred which they show towards these people all those who are full of 'humanitarianism', the so-called ladies of charity, who when you show them these pictures they rush to attack you for ...'populism' (!) use idiocy as a defence starting from the barricades of Northern Mykonos but talking about ...North Korea and they respond: **'We are Staying in Europe'**...

Ex Health Minister Georgiadis who presided over mass hospital closures cheering for …Europe

B. Eyewitness Reports: The Fall of Syriza

Syriza RIP

Tsipras: Too much energy result zero...
A lot of energy by the world's corporate media was placed
into Syriza. First with the pseudo image of the youth
rebellion of 2008 then the alleged participation in the
Squares Movement and in the last two years in cultivating
his image as the Chavez of Greece by an assortment of
dubious Ford Foundation outfits the world over.
If one takes into account the energy with the output ie
burning him in less than six months one is left with the idea
bourgeois politics is at an impasse...

On €50b Greek state assets to be parked in Brussels

All Greek Gas and Oil contracts now go to Germans that's where the €50b of state assets come from... Tsipras is the Greek version of Obama a created politician from scratch in 2006 when they shipped him in to be Mayor of Athens... Only a political tramp would resurrect political zombies like New Democracy and PASOK. Today its a disgrace to be Greek.

Historical roots of today's sellout
From Eurocommunism to ...Euro Merkelism
The political transformation of Syriza from its eurocommunist roots to a sister party of the CDU has to occur fast within 72hours.
From Berlinguer to Merkel in the time it takes to fly to Australia and back...
Political globalism fast track.
I am signing up.

On Varoufakis
Was shipped in by Tsipras to lead Syrizas economics team from Milios. He brought with him Eleni Panariti of World Bank fame (when she helped collapse Peru with Fujimori) and spent 5 months writing up MoU 3. Resigned just as it was being brought to Greek Parliament...

4th Reich goes 'Left'
The end of Syriza is just a new beginning...

Many years of energy was created in promoting Tsipras as an anti-austerity politician starting from almost a decade ago when Syrizas predecessor Sinaspismos didn't have much chance of getting into Parliament and they promoted this alleged young radical, from a well established family which made its money in the era of the Junta. All that energy was dissipated in less than 6 months when on a historic day 14th August (day of invasion of Cyprus in 1974) Syriza voted for the 3rd Occupation Bailout.

For the first time in Greek history a party that originated from the Left fought for state power. That hasn't happened before in the 100 year history of the Greek Left. Why did it happen now? There can be no other explanation as we aren't privy to the inner workings of political parties and we can only observe from afar, that it was all pre-agreed and pre-arranged from the beginning. What the political forces of the capitalist establishment could not achieve was needed to be achieved by Syriza in power. That explains Tsipras intransigence over the election of the President way back in December 2014. If in a few months time he had no ideological or other hang ups in governing on the backs of ND-PASOK why could he have not provided support to the President supported by ND?

Neoliberals in Disguise: 4th Reich goes 'Left'

Whilst a small book was produced way back at the end of 2013 with the title

'Syriza Neoliberals in Disguise'

http://www.amazon.co.uk/Syriza-Greece-Neo-Liberals-Eyewitness-Patriotic/dp/1495460541

with eyewitness reports about the actual role of Syriza during the strikes and occupations that could have brought down Samaras ND, the extent of the capitulation of Syriza was so immense and so ridiculous that one is left with the idea that **their primary role in life was to destroy once and for all any notion of a Left.** The Syriza bandwagon and cheerleaders who were so catholic in their support for Syriza's radicalism were just a cover for pure unadulterated globalism, a left veneer of the 4th Reich. Any criticism of Syriza was seen to be anathema. The worst supporters of Syriza abroad were the Anglo-Americans. Various individuals arrived in Athens during the elections labelling Tsipras the Chavez of the Meditterranean. The irony of the situation was that a reporter arrived from Venezuela who stated the situation as is.

Greece: Pressure on Syriza to Deliver
http://imfoccupationgreece.blogspot.co.uk/2015/04/greece-pressure-on-syriza-to-deliver.html

This was part of the propaganda to raise the profile so Tsipras could sell the 3rd MoU. Debt is a business and like any other business it requires marketing. That was the primary purpose of Syrizas globalist bandwagon, to sell the 3rd MoU and reduce the fallback.

OXI Referendum

Tsipras staying in power by ND-PASOK-Potami

Believing the propaganda from the oligarchic newsnetworks, Syriza took a gamble with the referendum which backfired. They expected a close call between the YES and OXI and Tsipras was visibly shaken when he stood on a platform in front of hundreds of thousands in

Athens. As reported by Varoufakis when the OXI won, he was in depression. No one believes by selling the debt burden of the 3rd MoU the Syriza chiefs aren't in the business of making a killing.

After all their integrated relationships since 1989 with the economic establishment have been previously well documented. What is so ridiculous is to believe where the 1st and 2nd Bailout/MoU failed that the 3rd one will succeed. There is even a saying for the occasion. If you keep on doing the same thing over and over and getting the same result but expecting a different one, then you must be dumb. The Syriza tops aren't dumb. They are well educated. So it isn't an issue of miscalculation, that the 'negotiations' didn't go according to plan etc. Politics is a business and the business of politics is maintaining the business even if everyone else goes to pot. Keeping your hand in the honeypot is what this is about.

When working class districts voted around 85% for OXI it reaffirmed that people wanted a break with the prison house of the EU. Thousands have died due to the policies of economic genocide. They were ready for rupture. The leadership was lacking.

Mass immigration flows for the 4th Reich
Cheap labour is all the rage in the EU alongside zero hours contracts etc. With the extension of the EU east and the adding of another 100 million citizens and the maintenance of a national currency in a whole series of countries e.g. Romania, Bulgaria, Poland, Hungary etc. a whole series of privatisations occurred whereby Greeks were replaced by eg Bulgarians (cleaning contracts in Ministry of Economics) and the aim has always been to reduce those Greeks that remain in work to Asian levels of pay, whilst

remaining in the EZ. This is pretty well known and clear, but the fake left and its adoption of mass immigration flows under guise of 'non discrimination' is just the fake left veneer of the 4th Reich. Indeed characteristic of the fraud perpetrated by Syriza is to place in key ministries rabid neo-liberals eg. Ministry of Defence and Foreign Ministry. The coalition with ANEL was agreed behind closed doors but everyone knew it was coming as the big bourgeoisie will always govern in Greece, they would never allow a fake left party totally on its own.

Whilst the Foreign Minister Kotzias produced a booklet called 'Patriotic Left' about how small countries can survive under globalisation in reality it was just propaganda as to how a small country can become an appendage of the 4th Reich appropriating leftwing labels for an extreme right wing course. National socialism in practice...

The Three Stooges...

Syriza made a massive hue and cry about closing down existing immigrant receptions centres as they were allegedly inhuman (whilst mass unemployment for Greeks and the 20k suicides due to the economic genocide programme wasn't) in order then to give the green light abroad that whoever arrives in Greece can move on as it is now officially a free for all. The tourist centre of Athens started to resemble a third world zone again and now Syriza was forced to reopen new 'reception' centres. Obviously these are all govt contracts and he who signs the deals obviously gets a cut. Despite alleging they could house and feed the planet and that they would have 'humane treatment' what would that mean in practice if 2m arrived in a single year? How could Greece cope? It couldn't and Syriza does not give a shit if the last heavy industry of Greece tourism is run to the ground, as long as they can deliver what the 4th Reich demands an oversupply of cheap and pliant labour.
(UN Population Division report states Germany requires 150m immigrants over a 50 years period approx. 3.6m annually just for a single EU country)

NATO Israel lovefest.
If there ever was a sign that Syriza is deeply neo-liberal and reactionary to the core is its foreign policy. It pretended it required a deal with Russia and China to break out of the economic logjam and Lafazanis Fake Left Platform played its part in this going on little trips to Russia allegedly cutting deals but not breaking any EU sanctions on the country and alleviating the hit Greek agriculture took. Instead they shipped over Ukraine's injured soldiers so they could recuperate in Greece's state hospitals that no longer serve the Greek poor.
Kotzias was seen singing songs with NATOs leaders, the butchers of Yugoslavia, Afganistan, Libya. Not even a fake lip service to an 'ethical foreign policy'. Just 4th Reich promoters, blatantly.

To crown it all off they signed a military pact with Israel for joint military exercises, in other words to allow Israeli military to train Greeks in shooting down unarmed protestors in cold blood.

KKE propping up Syriza

KKE pushed through the line of abstaining in the referendum, campaigned openly for keeping the Euro and during the vote for the 3rd Bailout abstained from filibustering it. Fools assume they can maintain their existence following the establishment due to their history. They don't realise that in this era if words don't match deeds, you disintegrate. You have no political reason to exist. This will become clearer as time goes by.

KKE goons defending Parliament with the riot police during 1st MoU

Fake Left Platform-Syriza in Disguise Mk2
Whilst Syriza used riot police to crush El Dorado anti-gold protestors and this was Lafazanis Ministry they went quiet. They changed their tune and were now concerned about peoples jobs in this foreign owned gold hedge fund which will destroy the eco climate of a tourist area in N. Greece.

Lafazanis who is an old school operator instrumental in the KKEs governing with New Democracy pretended he was opposed to the 3rd MoU voting against it over its different phases over the last month. The game was to try to keep Syriza intact as it voted the whole package. This he achieved and that was his role. No premature split, no real denunciation of Tsipras, Dragasakis just a show of political fraud. Now they are pretending they will create a new movement against the 3rd MoU a split that occurred just like in New Democracy when Kammenos (ANEL) broke away. They will be probably be joined by other so-called anti-MoU forces (Antarsya, Plan B, Drachma party) in other words a new mini Syriza which have globalism in their DNA. They assume people can keep on repeating the same mistake in other words, Syriza goes for new elections or stays in power with ND votes (immaterial how it occurs), mass privatisations occur in the ports, railways and airports plus mass evictions for mortgage defaults and people will rally to a new anti-MoU front, elect it so that it eventually pushes through the ...4th Bailout.

There is no point in elections. People used Syriza to get rid of ND-PASOK. They then voted in the OXI referendum under conditions of 24/7 propaganda, under capital controls and under the threat of closing all banks indefinitely and paying zero pensions. Abstention is already around 40%. New elections will solve nothing. They are pointless. Abstention could reach +60%

What Next?
Parliamentarism is reaching its impasse. The longer it continues in this form makes it absolutely pointless. Since the mass protests of 2011 which destroyed the two main bourgeois parties ND-PASOK and brought Syriza into the political vacuum created, we are now entering totally unchartered waters. Merkels EU burnt Syriza so quickly that one assumes they cannot be that politically dumb. Syriza cannot remain in power in its present form, it is imploding. GD is in a self-imposed political exile that serves its purpose as it doesn't seek or desire political

power and the KKE sounds and talks that it has just arrived from another planet.

The new struggles forced on Greek farmers and workers with the new round of economic cuts will create new political conditions and a new situation. Court martialling workers and breaking strikes using law courts and the riot police (as Samaras ND did) alone will be hard to swallow taking into account no other political formation exists on the horizon that will take the situation left. But without a fighting left from the ground up there will be nothing …left.

Greek history does not start or end with Syriza, it's end is just a new beginning.

Meimarakis ND and Tsipras Syriza

Updates Elections 2015

6th August
Zoi Konstantopoulou to create her own political formation
Despite its best intentions Syriza could not become
PASOK.
The ex Left Platform won't become Syriza.
History is destroying bourgeois politics not encouraging
them.
Syriza was a shell of an organisation even when it won
37% in the last elections. Now resignations are occurring
up and down the country.
Careerists will join Laiki Enotita to prepare themselves for
the 4th bailout.
It took a decade to create Syriza and 6months to destroy it.
The ferocity of the capitalist onslaught implies nothing is
politically solid anymore and won't be either for the
foreseeable future...

27th August
Lafazanis is insisting elections constitutionally cannot
occur until one month after today which is correct. Tsipras
wants to rush them to minimise his losses
Tsipras gave fake interview on Alpha stating that he wont
govern with other parties after the elections.
Lafazanis called for the abolition of the 50 MP bonus
which was Syriza policy, but it wont occur.
Zoi Konstantopoulou claimed she will create her own
political party.

28th August
Fake polls giving Laiki Enotita 3.5% and PASOK 4%...

Tsipras to run campaign against old establishment whilst he was governing with them the last two months...and he can only stay in power with them.
No polls show abstention showing how bent they are.
Fake miners in Skouries blocking roads.
Ship owners doing daily trips shipping tens of thousands of illegals into the EU.

29th August

You are all rotten shouts protester as
eggs are thrown at Lapavitsas in Kavala sq just before public meeting of Laiki Enotita. People assume they are all the same as they didn't split prior to 3rd Bailout when they had the chance. Clowns
4k illegals arrive in one night in Lesvos.
All squares are full of tents.

30th August

Lafazanis went on a stroll in Lesvos said nothing, but supports Open Border with Turkey
Essentially saying it all looks good.

31st August

EPAM Kazakis to stand independently
Antarsya split standing independently, Garganas won't go with Lafazanis due to previous deed in DEA being there.
OKDE standing
EEK WRP Savvas Michael probably standing.
All as usual pointless, no one abstaining when abstention will go through the roof.
Don't know if the party of hunters are standing. Or Movement Can't Pay or Won't Pay

2-3rd September
Tsipras held pre electoral meeting in square in Agaleo, a couple of thousand were there.
All polls show Syriza getting around 20%. During referendum all polls were out by a quarter. Theoretically Syriza could dip below 10% in one go.
Main argument now is he won't govern with New Democracy.

5th September
Meimarakis the ND leader said we need a broad based govt.
Polls now show 7 parties will pass 3% threshold to get in.
ANEL Kammenos produce electoral spot showing Tsipras being left handed but being taught to sign with his ...right.
Douzinas globalist clown in Syriza but based in London to become a Syriza MP now they are Merkelites.

7th September
Discussion has moved on now to alliances.
Tsipras states won't be alliances with ND hinting at PASOK and Potami.
Wishful thinking that PASOK will survive.
ND hints at governing with Syriza. Some polls show Syriza only retaining 60% of its electoral base. ND assumes it can win back lost supporters. Wishful thinking. Abstention appears in polls for first time at 40%. Hence +55% likely outcome.

12th September
Reports are circulating that if there is +51% abstention the first party that wins doubles its number of elected MP's!!

Victor Orban Hungarys PM demands the EU sends an army to Greece under guise of stopping pseudo refugee influx.
Sofia Sakorafa Syriza Euro MP left the party.
Syriza ND in the UN vote on debt restructuring for poor countries voted against it, proving once and for all that all their talk about debt restructuring was hot air alongside the fake committees set up to investigate it...

15th September
2nd TV debate with Tsipras Meimarakis in the backdrop of Skouries miners protesting outside ERT TV station
ND still promoting govt between Syriza ND. Tsipras allegedly still holding out trying to maintain his electoral base. Asked if he would gover with PASOK Potami hinted that he would.
Tsipras main bone of contention is not allowing GD to become official opposition stating essentially that if people don't vote for Syriza GD will rise.

If Germany closes its borders Greece will be left with hundreds of thousands in every city to look after even when they cant look after themselves...

17th September
GDs leader Mihaloliakos realising his party may get more votes than expected stated he accepts the political killing of Fissas. Said nothing about the murder of two or his supporters. An establishment figure who not long ago like the KKE came out in support of the Euro and the EU he plays the retro fascist card to appear anti establishment.

18th September

Mass corporate media for the first time are mentioning abstention that it's going to be higher than usual ie 40% Could be as much as 55 or 70%.

Farmers announced road blockades on Sunday and islands facing the double whammy of increased VAT and mass immigration inflows may also boycott the elections as a protest.

C. Economic Issues (EU/EZ, Debt and national economy)

Since the street occupations and protests of 2010-11 the issue of the Drachma has started to dominate public political life. The corporate news media embedded to the social structures of the 4th Reich ran a massive campaign during the struggle for the referendum that the real question of the referendum was Drachma or Euro. The started street protests which also went to the top front of Parliament and Syria did not stop them. When anti-Troika protestors tried that over the years they were teargassed to hell and beaten to smithereens and back. The first attempt at storming Parialiament were by PAME members and they were accused as being Nazi by their leadership who label any action they don't control as being either infiltrated by Nazis or run by security service.

Syriza promised E751 minimum wage, they also promised E12k minimum tax threshold and an unemployment supplement with housing for the long term unemployed. All good on paper, but as Tsakalotos who came to the British Parliament argued we will defend the Euro at all costs.

Infront of a cross party parliamentary representation he stated quite bluntly there never was a progressive critique of the single currency, all critiques were from the far right. This from a man who spent the 1980's in Thatcher's Britain and obviously knew the arguments around EMU. After all he had written feasibility studies with Stournaras (central economic bankster of Greece) with respect to Greece and the single currency so he had a lot of political capital invested in that project. Just from his look and tone of his voice one could sense he wasn't interested in the plight of Greek people just about the plight of maintaining relationships with the EU, selling debt and taking a cut.

The main argument that if we left the EZ and the EU the world would cave in etc was constantly on 24/7. Alongside the engineered capital controls they were used as tool to get people to vote YES in the referendum, which didn't actually work and represents a massive shift in consciousness. Greek pensioners no longer influence voting intentions as they did in 2012.

The other big myth is that Greece produces nothing and if left the EZ it would disintegrate completely becoming a European version of Somalia. Such is the pro-EU quislingness of the modern day Merkelists that they assume their fearmongering frightens people.

It doesn't and the referendum showed that clearly as despite the mass propaganda that it was really a referendum about the Euro vs Drachma how come the Drachma won? The other debate is that the KKE has once more come out against the return of the Drachma claiming it's a conspiracy amongst domestic capital vs foreign.

Varoufakis has emerged as an anti-austerity bailout individual when everyone knows he has close relations with Panariti (World Bank fame during infamous period of Fujimoris rule in Peru) and was an adviser to Papandreou during first bailout was Finance Minister of Greece during 3rd Bailout and the only characteristic of him is that he has big backers as nothing sticks the Teflon don of Greek finance who in six months as Greek finance minister implemented not one iota of the now infamous Thessaloniki programme.

Prior to the emergence of Alavanos Plan B and Katsanevas Drachma party an article appeared on the issue of the Drachma vs Euro which was included in the book How the IMF broke Greece covering the debates around the role and purpose of a national currency and clearly setting the left case for exit from the EZ/EU. Greek society has moved on and now the views regarding a return to a national currency are widespread and after the emergence of capital controls in the summer of 2015 all that was lacking was the political will for a break up of monetary union. Without a return to a national currency there never will be an attempt at returning to an economy which has elements of control, control of the banking system so investments can occur in production which is geared to maximize value and provide jobs to the 2m unemployed. A socialist exit from the crisis becomes the only possible solution and will be a product of necessity not ideology, going left is a matter of national survival, but its geopolitical implications are larger than the actors involved as it will heralds a collapse of the EZ and subsequently an unraveling of the EU. That is why Grexit gains so much importance.

Drachma vs Euro

For the corrupt mass media a return to the Drachma equals destruction! For what reason they don't say. It is served as an honour and explanations don't exist. It is destruction, because it is ...destruction, pure an simple!

"Catastrophic for Greece was how it was characterised by a journalist Ev Mitilinaios the scenario of returning to the drachma" we read in the VIMA newspaper, without anywhere the argument being justified.

The same goes for Papariga (leader of the KKE) who actually doesn't tire in warning us:"A return to the drachma under the current conditions would be catastrophic"!
The why and how must be held only for themselves.

Also the European specialists speak about destruction but we understand them eg. The president of the European central bank, Z. C. Trichet who supports that it will be: destructive for the Eurozone the return to the drachma. He doesn't say this for Greece. We would agree with him, with the meaning that a departure of Greece from the Eurozone, would mean the end of an opportunist, stupid and criminal attempt to impose a united currency without a united economy and state. The responsibility belongs to the architects of the EU and the Eurozone, with the victim being Greece and the other countries of the European South.

There are others who state that due to the lack of a similar experience, the honest reply to the question as to 'what will happen if we return to the drachma' is simply, 'I don't know'!

We Have Experience

In reality there is experience not from one but many countries. Typically they aren't the same, but essentially they don't differ. Before we analyse things more, let us give a hypothetical preliminary example so one can be better understood:
Let us assume we had held onto the drachma but had latched it onto a hard currency, something which isn't at all rare in international practice, eg the Euro. Whoever gave us one drachma we would give them back one euro. That is what happened in the beginning of the 1990's with the Argentinian peso. So as to be confronted, they said, inflation, would be added to the dollar. One peso=one dollar and the opposite. This occurred with the bright sparks down at the IMF!

The results are well known.

The problem of the Argentinian economy was found in its currency? A big deceipt. A case of fetischism, which we come across only in the field of religion. Where the painter of holy images paints Mary and falls down on his feet in front of his piece of art and asks for himself to be saved! Thus man in society and commercial production has lot from his eyes his true relationships with his co-citizens and the division of labour among them, due to common survival and fantasizes that his life is determined not by the relationship with his co-workers but by other creations eg from a printed piece of paper, like the peso, which in and of itself has minimal value.

The diagnosis is wrong and the medicine chosen also. The patient wasn't the typed piece of paper as is always to be believed by monetarist bourgeois economics but in the given situation the low level of competition of the Argentinian economy in the international arena. The medicine chosen for the peso to become as hard as the dollar, without having in the background the dynamism of the US economy, the only thing it could achieve was to destroy totally the competitiveness of the Argentinian economy. As exactly happened.

Argentinan had to travel backwards, its peoples had to suffer for a decade, to go bankrupt essentially for 75% of the debt to be written off, to disconnect the peso from the dollar and for it to be devalued, for the economy to start to develop once more. Naturally the problem wasn't solved permanently as the Argentinian economy is part of the world economy and in conditions of world crisis they cannot but influence all the national economies. The abandonment of the policy of the hard currency in Argentina ended up being the correct and imposed choice.

With Greece before WW2 the same had occurred. Venizelos as well in the name of anti-inflationary targets, latched the drachma onto the British pound and later onto the dollar. As a result imports made money instead of exports, the deficits grew alongside the debts. Venizelos (no relation to current Economics Minister!) responded with an intensification of direct taxation, with sackings, cuts, autarchy and violence. In 1932 the country was forced to declare bankruptcy, taking the drachma off the link with the dollar and devaluation. Due to the policy that he followed the Liberal party imploded and Venizelos was forced to junk in his political career. From his ridiculous insistence on the hard drachma the political duet of Glyxbourg (ex-King) – Metaxas whilst the dictatorship that followed led the borrowers that Greece would continue to pay its debts.

Like Argentina in our days, Greece not only did not destroy itself, as the pre-war Cassandras predicted but with a weapon the national monetary policy and its refusal to continue to pay this odious debt, it added phenomenal rhythms of development taking on the third highest on the planet after Japan and the Soviet Union!

What is the difference of coming out of a link with whatever hard currency (or from the hard Euro – if that was the relationship) from the forced or chosen exit from the Eurozone? None whatsoever. Let them not say that there isn't a historical parallel that we don't have experience and we don't know what the consequences are going to be for a return to our national currency.

I have referred to two examples but there are tens of others. Let those who sell catastrophism sell it it to those who have no clue. We will not allow Greece and the Greek nation to disappear so some can sell slavery to the Euro-atlantic bosses defending either which way the condemned Eurozone.

UNFOUNDED CATASTROPHIST SYLLOGISMS

In the press and the internet one finds syllogisms against the return of the drachma, but one doesn't find many arguments. That isn't a coincidence. I haven't searched extensively but to the extent that I did, I found four paragraphs by Petros Dukas with which he tries to convince us that a return to the Drachma will be catastrophic. For all those that don't realise relatively that he was Deputy Minister in two New Democracy govts, he studied economics and international relations in George Washington University, company management and finance economics at Columbia University and economics in New York University, to which he became a doctor of Economics. He also worked for Citibank in New York and became the general manager for the same bank in Greece.

P. Dukas supports that:
"The discussion and the threatening dilemma for a return to the drachma is unintelligible and self-destructive for our country.
Further down he posts the first attack we will be forced to accept as Greeks!
The points numbered are Dukas the answers are mine.

1) We will constitute acceptance that us Greeks have totally failed, that we are unable to compete and we are in the 3rd Division of Europe
Us Greeks were never asked or questioned if they wanted Greece to become a member of the EEC. Any who had a

basic understanding knew that Greece was being thrown into a wolves den, as without trade protectionism it was impossible to compete with the west-European mega giants, when essentially , without the nations being asked, the rule of common market preference on the basis which the Union occurred, never functioned as this is how the uncontrolled centres of power in Brussels decided. Even worse there never were any European trade boundaries. With the GATT agreements and later the WTO ones the European market was transformed officially into a united world market, without the nations being asked. The entrance of Greece in 2001 into the Eurozone was the last nail in the coffin of the Greek economy. The fate of the Greek economy had been judged and that was known by all our politicians (amongst which is Dukas) unless of course we are to accept they are chosen simply by the level of dumbness.

2) The 'New Drachma' would unavoidably become immensely devalued in order to be able to aid the competitiveness of our exports. But never before has devaluation had anything more than medium term successes. It led to a cycle of inflation, a fear of a new devaluation, exit of capital and finally new devaluations.

Above the doctor of economics and deputy minister of economics (let us not forget that one) tells us that "we failed totally, that we are unable to become competitive and we are falling into the 3rd Division" But in paragraph 2 we accepted that the devalued drachma will "aid the competitiveness of exports" and consequently accepts that the overvalued for Greek measures euros will undermine our competitiveness. This doesn't stop him arguing (totally illogically) that the return of the drachma is destruction! He must assume that he is talking to idiots…

FEAR MONGERING NONSENSE

Where does it come from that the devalued drachma equals inflation? Or that more inflation brings about more inflation and that is why we will have capital flight abroad? All of this isn't but nonsense with which our esteemed Dr. is trying to frighten the people.

Inflation develops when we have few goods in the market in relation with demand hence we have an increase in prices. Or when the country is forced to print money from air as it has created obligations where its actual government coffers aren't able to service.

The new drachma will be devalued in relation not to itself but from its original price 1Euro=340.75Drachma s which it was on 1st January 2001. Not because it is written in its DNA but because it is to the interest of the country. It must because Greece became an open border paradise and lost all its rights handed over to foreign centres of power with the Euro hanging on its neck and lost as a result 50% of of its competitiveness.

There will be repercussion which will occur on life, but they will only be positive. If the German Euro can't be devalued for the Greek terrain, the quislings that rule us found the answer in devaluing our lives. How else are we going to feed the usurers and we save the eurozone which is one step away from death! They are taking the last cent which is circulating in the country having provoked a depression, mass unemployment, they cut and cut again salaries, pensions, they have unleashed a fierce tax chasing mechanism, the make incessant and constant increases in fuel, the prices of all utilities, the prices of all the basic basket of goods, they destroy the welfare state, all the services linked to people, health, education, everything.

The "New Drachma" which will replace the Euro will have the same form one euro = one new drachma which should become a paper note, with the same subdivisions and paper multipliers so as to avoid whatever speculation against the consumers. Whatever could be bought with one euro should be bought with one drachma. A wage of 800 Euros will become a wage of 800drachmas. The necessary devaluation is related to the relationship of the drachma with the euro and foreign currencies. In 2001 it was 1E=340drachma. Due to the economic meltdown which the country has suffered whose fault is due to the corrupt political personnel this relationship will change in defence of the drachma if we want to promote our exports and tourism. 1 Euro can become = 440.75drachmas. This devaluation in relation to foreign currencies is obviously going to influence to an extent the internal prices of the market, but not in a country where the govt will utilise all the possibilities internally and our relationships with abroad. We must add that a return to a drachma on its own does not satisfy for the country to stand on its feet. It must constitute the beginning of a new course, the independent and national domination of Greece, ready for new openings and open to fruitful cooperations with new peoples all over the planet, on the basis of mutual gain alone.

To proceed further: which exit of capital and fear of inflation is Dukas talking about? There are around $350 billion euros and dollars in the bank of Greece. There are the trading reserves of the country and not one has the right to touch them. If the state has the will it is in the position of defending them. Let us forget about capital flight. Neither Argentina in our days nor Greece in 1932 confronted such issues with bankruptcy and will not confront them now. The planet as a whole is facing the most complicated the most explosive crisis in its history and there are no areas which are now secure for any currency in any country. If capital flight occurs in Turkey which has its own currency the same will occur in Greece...

3) The massive debt in Euros should be paid in devalued drachmas. As a result our debt will increase to around 250% of GDP!
Will the doctor of economics drive us mad: Given the fact that the 'massive debt' won't anyway be paid back (everyone understands that) not only is the debt transformed into drachmas but so does the GDP. Therefore the relationship of debt to GDP, remains constant, it doesn't change because we change currency.

4) All the citizens with investments and deposits in our country would aim to avoid the losses incurred from a return to a Drachma and would take out quickly all the capital abroad with the result being the immediate collapse of the banking system and economic activity!

The respect and worth of a currency of a country is determined by the productivity of work but also by the quality of the productive goods. It improves or deteriorates from the development of these two factors. If they impose a currency on you like the Euro whose respectability and its price in the markets is very high as it is based on German competitiveness and quality, then it is truly illogical and an unnatural situation as it weakens severely exports, as he accepts in the 2nd paragraph and supports imports. With the

Euro Greece has a permanent date with bankruptcy. We need a 180degree turn and one of the first measures for the country on the road to development is a return to a cheap drachma. When that occurs we wont have capital flight or investments from the country. The New Democracy 'doctor of economics' deceives aims to influence the Greek people. With the cheap drachma capital will flood into the country. If the opposite occurred as is being alleged we wouldn't see American and European capital emigrating to China with the cheap Renminbi but Chinese, Korean and Taiwanese to be emigrating to Western Europe and the USA!

As for the banks we say going bankrupt one after the other from the epidemic in the USA and Un Kingdom that occurred not because of capital flight abroad (so as to find safe ports, where truly?) but because we have a lack of liquidity, as their reserves are 'toxic' they are obligations by debtors who cannot pay. That is why every now and again states are making injections of liquidity in the banks so as to keep alive the money of its citizens. That occurs because it is in the nature of the market (which has been deliberately deified) cutting things down to size or increasing as it sees fit. The market is a creation of man and his creation, it cannot regulate the life of its creator. The creator man will tomorrow regulate the market and thus his life.

www.patari.org
August 2011

The EU and Greece: Who Props up Who?

Junquer head of Euro Group Greeces problems started 30 years ago...

Greek Trade Deficits
1980 till 2008 Greece's trade deficit with the rest of the world went up 9 times
In current prices from £5.2b in 1980 it reached E44b in 2008 and E34b in 2009
In 1980 Greece had a surplus in its farming budget at 3.3b Drachmas but from 1981 the year it first joined the EU it went to a deficit to E290m. The deficit has now gone to E3b Euros an increase of 934%

Foreign Loans by Years
Foreign loans taken out in 1990 were equivalent to E694m
In 2000 equivalent to E7.16b
In 2009 equivalent to E85b
So by 2009 the Greeks were 1,009% more in debt than in 2000 (decade of the Euro!!)
Public Debts
In 1980 it was E600m
Three decades later it was E298b
The debt went up 497times in joining the EU

EU 'AID' to GREECE
Four major packages
-1986-1993 for E471m
-1994-1999 E12.3b

2000-2006 E26.1b
2007-2013 E27b
If one aggregates them all they equal to about **E65b**
In a period of 33years from the joining the EU Greeks
'received' 'aid packages' equivalent to 196Euros a year or
0.54c a day!

Greece's Trade Deficits with the EU

Imports equivalent to E379b for the three decades of
entrance
Exports equivalent to E125b
Conclusion we gave them E254b for imports received E65b
in 'aid'.
In other words for every Euro we received we gave back 5
Christine Lagarde = Greece's Deficits are Germany's
Surpluses Oct 2010

Taken from the Greek book Ειναι ο Καπιταλισμος Ηλιθιε
"Its Capitalism Stupid" Nick Bogiopoulos

The Economics of Genocide

Made in Greece by IMF-EU

The depression and the MoU (memorandum of understandings) have evaporated around 65Billion Euros in relation to 2008. During the same period the govts cut around 23billion Euros whilst investments were reduced by 2/3 and the consumer demands of households reduced by 36billion Euros.

The numbers show with clarity the 'miracles' performed in Greece in the last 5-6 years from the governments of both parties who are demanding once more our vote to complete their destructive work in cooperation – during periods – in cooperation with other (vanished political forces like LAOS and Dem Left) but they surely don't describe the extent of the humanitarian catastrophe which was implemented in the name of efficiency and growth.

The statistics produced by the Greek statistical body could be referred to as 'Statistics of Genocide' as they constantly remind us that no horrific achievement no new tragedy will stop the disastrous policies of the coalition govts in charge. A policy they follow with frightening regularity all these years towards the advantage of the banks, the big construction companies, the ship owners, the big tax evaders, the 'investors' etc

None of these give anything to the unemployed and with the semi unemployed constitute around 1.5 million with 1 million positions being lost, the strangulation of the welfare state and the destruction of hundreds of thousands of small businesses.

GDP

In 2013 the GDP was reduced in relation to 2008 by E65b Euros or by a percentage of 26% (It was 25% during the Greek civil war which only lasted 3 years!) The percentage as well as the duration of the crisis are profound for the western world during the post war period.

In the same period wages were reduced by 23b or by 28% whilst the consumer spending of households was reduced by 36b Euros or by a percentage of 22%> Investments were reduced by 37b Euros or by 65%

Industrial Production and Consumer Sales

Last October industrial production was 24% reduced in relation to the same month as 2008

The volume of consumer sales was reduced by 35% in relation to the same month as 2008

In relation to sales in stores we notices the following reductions:

-Big supermarkets by 26%.

-Food, drinks, smoke -35%

-Chain stores by -43%

-Fuel -34%.

-Clothes -50%.

-Furniture household items -50%

Employment-Unemployment

In this sector are to be found some of the 'best' achievements of the current government

In the 3rd quarter of 2014 there were 3.6m in work 1m less th an in the same period of 2008. A reduction of 22%

In the same period official unemployment increased from 355k to 1.3m ie around 900k

If we add those 250k in number who work so little that they appear to be more like the unemployed then the unemployed are around 1.5m

Let's look now at the losses in the most important sectors of the economy in the 3rd quarter of 2014 in relation to 2008.

-Agriculture -30k or 6%

-Restaurants 230k or 42%

-Construction 240k or 60%.

-Trade 200k or -24%

-Transport -43k or -20k.

-Tourism -2,900 1%

-Banks, insurance companies -28k or 24%

-Public administration, defence, social security 65k -17%

-Εκπαίδευση -34.100. -10,8%.

-Education -34k -10%

-Health -21k or 9%

The 'family basket'

The median spend of the Greek family has been reduced to 1.5k Euros from 2.3k Euros in 2009. In other words inside of four years it has been reduced by 30% or around 700Euros

Greek households reduced their spend on food by 17.5% whilst they have stopped essentially spending money on clothes and shoes by 50%

The smallest drops have been the costs for education or more importantly private education as they were reduced even more than the reductions for food by about 17%. Greeks chose to eat less but to ensure their children continued their education

After the reductions for food we had reductions in health by 20% or drinks by 27% or housing by 30% hotels and eating in restaurants by 38% and transport by 40% (purchase of cars, fuel etc)

Social Protection

The Troika hit with particular venom against the welfare state using Presidential Decrees extreme neoliberal practices but in particular the vile attacks against the social groups which had some form of social protection and the dissolution of all the networks of social protection.

Based on ELSTATs figures which only go up to 2012 (we do not have those for the extreme 2013) we are placing the main social welfare policies and how they developed to 2012 from 2009. They all develop negatively with the possible exception of pensions where here it appears the cost has increased not because pensions increased but because of the large number of people that went for early retirement.

Social benefits in millions of Euros				
	2009	2012	difference	%
Mothers benefit	470	400	-70	-14,9%
Family Benefits	722	552	-170	-23,5%
Pregnancy benefit	100	48	- 52	-52,0%
Pension benefits	16.876	21.287	4.411	26,1%
Health benefits	1.102	1.010	- 92	-8,3%
Hospital care	7.588	5.270	-2.318	-30,5%
Care outside hospitals	7.838	5.110	-2.728	-34,8%
Unemployment pay	1.611	1.423	-188	-11,7%
Disability pensions	1.515	1.276	-239	-15,8%

Looking at the chart until 2012 that is we see that whilst unemployment has increased by 250% unemployment pay has been reduced by 12%. (Unemployment is only paid for a short period of time and then nothing is provided) At the same time by 52% the benefits for birth are reduced in a country where deaths outnumber births.

Hospital treatments have been reduced by a third and disability pensions by 16% whilst family benefits have been reduced by 25%

Between 2009 and 2012 costs were reduced by 5.3b Euros or around 8.5%

Only total pensions have shown an increase of 13%

In other areas of social protection the situation has developed accordingly

·   Illness 6K million -32%

·   Disability -395million -13.5%

·   Widow -550m -10%

·   Family 1k million -25%

·   Unemployment -56m -1.5%

·   Housing -677million Euros -58%

·   Social Care 112m Euros-112 -8,3%.

If in 5 years of Troika austerity around 25-30% of the economy is shattered another 5 years of this and there won't be any economy left to realistically talk about.

"The greatest violence is that of being Sacked or Unemployed"

Greece: They Destroyed Us and Now Want the Bones

Whom did the ruling economic interests ask when they put us into the EEC? **No one.** The Left in that era screamed and warned: Greece out of the Lions Den! They understood then that the victors in WW2 has decided to implement the Nazi plan for the unification of Europe under the iron heel of big business, in alliance with the local collaborators in each country.

They abolished economic borders in Greece, services, and for people and goods without asking us. They dismissed us and demand sacrifices from us. Even our lives. They abolished our borders not to turn Asia into Europe but to turn Europe into Asia, with its people's and the working Greek into an unemployed beggar left on the sidelines! Who apart from Euro and American grovellers. The political families Karamanlides, Mitsotakides,Simitides, Samarades, Venizeloi and other parasites who enriched themselves with our impoverishment. On the other hand the Left which hasn't capitulated like the KKE which wavers towards the big construction bosses and the sold out trade unionists they who ally themselves directly with German and European interests.

From the moment where the great European powers transformed once again without asking the European Nations, the European Economic Community to the European Union with the Euro as a common currency and the Greek economy (not only the Greek) became a totally open shop without any element of monetary, trade or other form of protectionism, so it was inevitable to transform the country into a massive trade deficit which would constantly increase and the country would be condemned to a total bankruptcy and destruction. This is the date imposed on us by the big european powers have the gall to ask us for its bones instead of compensating us for the destruction and the deaths they provoked. The political powers in Greece threw the Greek people into the Lion's Den, provoking a massive destruction to the country and its people to serve big foreign interests so as they benefit accordingly, must give explanations and they will for their crimes.

The Greek people never borrowed anything and owe nothing to nobody. Instead they are victim of exploitation by the big 'allied' powers. For the reconstruction of the country and development and in order to be able to have a despicable standard of living must become master of its own country, with borders for persons, for products, and with our national currency the Drachma. All the country and its wealth which has been created must be controlled by its people who shed blood sweat and tears creating it. There is no room for compromise and retreat. It's time for all sides to understand this.

www.patari.org

Dollar vs Euro
Manipulated Euro Crisis to Prop up Ailing Dollar via Greece?

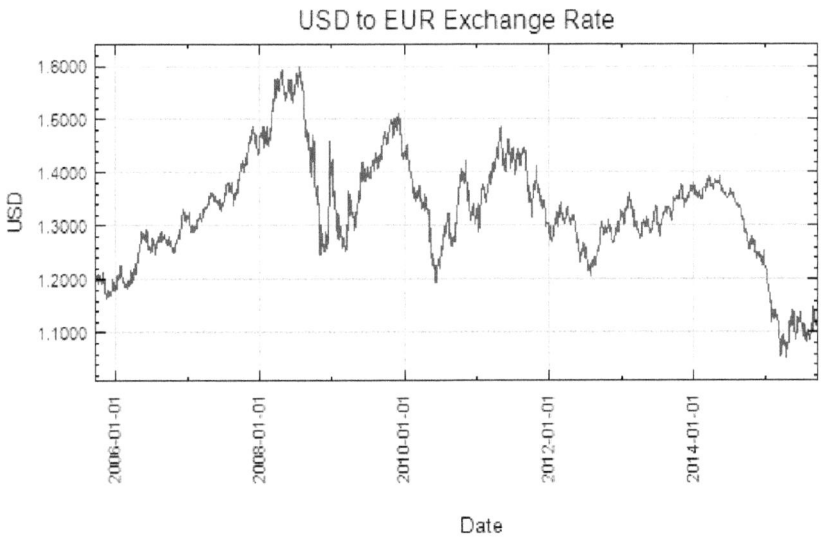

During 2007/8 Dollar was historically weak in relation to Euro losing 60% in value.
Then Euro Crisis starts with all significant peaks and troughs being related to Greece
The biggest internal devaluation of any member state hit Greece with highest mass unemployment.
Dollar dropped throughout 2011 increased in value when Goldman Sachs boy Papadimos came to power in February 2012.

Dollar to depreciate again during during mid 2013-mid 2014 so this is period when Tsipras went to Texas and announced he would fight for power (Nov 2013). Tsipras assumes power and Dollar at historic highs (in relation to Euro) with 50m on food stamps in USA. (2015) Dollar has appreciated 60% with Euro in relation to 2007/8.

Alavanos placed Tsipras in his position. Who is Tsipras? A political non entity who returned from his trip to Texas and suddenly wanted power. The Greek Left has never sought power in the entirety of its history. So why now? With the IMF in the EU and the constant conflicts between Greece and Germany the Euro is influenced downward. Grexit is not on the political agenda, never has been by any existing political formation

VN Gelis

Syriza Has No Plan B

Wednesday, 20 May 2015 *Joshua Tartakovsky*, *Truthout | Interview*

Syriza leader Alexis Tsipras at a press conference during the 77th International Fair in Thessaloniki, Greece. (Photo: Ververidis Vasilis / Shutterstock.com**)**

Truthout combats corporate power by bringing you trustworthy, independent news. Join our mission by making a donation now!

We live in times when national sovereignty is being eroded in favor of global capital. Syriza plans to continue with austerity and has made no serious plan B. All actions taken so far reveal that Syriza intends to continue with the austerity program and in the summer Greece will probably sign a new contract of continued austerity.

The question remains whether the people will rise against the loss of sovereignty. This interview was conducted on April 1, 2015, with Dimitris Kazakis, leader of the United

Popular Front (E.PA.M). The party opposes austerity and was founded in 2011 by people who participated in anti-memorandum demonstrations in Greece. Kazakis is a socialist economist who worked in the private sector in the past.

The interview has been amended and shortened.

Joshua Tartakovsky: Do you think that the current government has some kind of plan B in mind or are they just trying their best?

Dimitris Kazakis: I don't think they even have a plan A. In the first week after the elections, they tried some general idea, like the European Convention on debt issues. The European Union rejected it so they [the Greek government] abandoned the whole idea.

On the second level, they tried to negotiate some kind of elimination of debt, but nobody wanted it, and they did not want to go into a confrontation with the lenders, so they lost ground. Since the agreement of February 20, the Greek government abided by the rules of the loan agreement.

The agreement of February 20 had contradictions in it. It was obvious from the beginning that Greece could not satisfy both the troika and the people. Still, the fact that [Prime Minister Alexis] Tsipras brought the issue of reparations from Germany for the World War II occupation seemed to suggest that he is trying to mobilize the people.

If you see the declarations, you will find out that according to Tsipras and his government, the German reparations are not a legal issue between Germany and Greece, but an ethnical issue. The way Tsipras is pushing the German reparations issue is to close it.

But why would he bring up the question of reparations in the first place? Is Prime Minister Tsipras not seeking to effect some kind of confrontation?

Because of the people. The Greek people expected too much from the new government. And they have to put up a theater performance for the Greek people. So that the average Greek citizen can say, "Let's wait for three or four months to see what is going on with the government," because the government and the media say they should wait for three or four months because then people will see that there will be a confrontation in midsummer. I don't think there will be a confrontation. In midsummer, we will see the signing of a new agreement. We are going for the worse.

Mr. Tsipras has been complaining that the Eurogroup is holding him to higher standards, not even to the standards of the new Eurogroup agreement, but to standards of the memorandum of understanding from the time of [Antonis] Samaras ...

Yes. He says that. But give me an example of the propositions that the Greek government gave to the Eurogroup that are outside of the commitments that were already signed in April 2014 in the last memorandum.

What they are trying to do is to convince the people that by doing that, by fulfilling the commitments of the last policy, they are changing policy. That is nonsense.

Still, the government must know that if it continues in the same path of austerity, its political future is finished. So why would it commit suicide like that?

They will create a new government [and break up with the left flank of Syriza, JT], a national coalition government, with To Potomi, with parts of Pasok and New Democracy and with Golden Dawn, saying that there is no other way.

But Syriza must know that they won't be voted in again if they continue with the same austerity.

Yes, but I think that they might create a special situation here in Greece in order for the people to be frightened and probably they will form a national unity or interim government like the Papademos government we had in 2012.

The actions Mr. [Yanis] Varoufakis seems to be taking in favor of remaining in the euro do not match what he describes in his book, THE GLOBAL MINOTAUR, on the failure of capitalism. How do you explain this?

Mr. Varoufakis has a position that didn't alter since 2011. The main position is that you can forget about Greece, because either you can have a European solution or no solution. So whatever you say or whatever you analyze, when it comes to choosing which way to go, actually he will chose - because he believes it - the European way. And there is no way inside the eurozone to find a solution, especially for Greece.

Greece could get finances through Russia or China or even the US ...

Well, yes. We have more than a 324 billion euro public debt and we are paying each year around 30 billion in monetization of that debt. Who is going to give us the money? Nobody. Why would they?

> **"You have to start from repudiating the debt. Saying that 'you know, you made us less than a colony.'"**

For example, if you get rid of the debt and say goodbye to the euro, you can go to Russia or China and say, "Can you supplement our currency deposits for our exterior balance?" They will probably say, "OK, let's discuss. I can give you the money; what can you give me?" But inside the eurozone, Russia and China know that they cannot provide directly to the government itself. They must negotiate through Berlin or Brussels.

How much support do you think Tsipras has within Syriza if he were to sign a new austerity memorandum?

In my opinion, Tsipras has control of around 55 percent of his own MPs.

Would they agree to the next memorandum?

That's why they don't want the agreement of February 20 to go through parliament. They are frightened of their own MPs voting against it.

What do you see as a possible solution to the current crisis?

In my opinion, you have to get rid of the euro and declare the repudiation of debt. You have to start from repudiating the debt. Saying that "you know, you made us less than a colony."

But what would you do to prevent speculation against the drachma? Capital flight?

First of all, we have to implement capital controls. It's not a big deal; in Cyprus you see how even the European Bank put in capital controls, of course in favor of the big capital in Cyprus. We can do it in favor of the Greek economy and of course in favor of the majority of the Greek people. At the same time, there will be no speculations because we need around six to eight months to import the new national currency and for the first six to eight months we will have the euro. Who is going to speculate against the euro?

But the day the drachma comes in, there will be speculation.

To speculate against the national currency, you have to find it first freely in the foreign markets. Give me one reason, for the new government and the state's central bank, to place the new currency in the foreign markets? We are not going to support foreign speculation by selling our new national currency. We can say that after two years, there will be a meeting for stabilization and development of the Greek economy and then we will make our national currency available for purchase only by those who want to buy our currency for more than 4 billion euros.

"We can have higher wages every year when we invest in the productivity of labor, not in the price of the labor."

That's the good thing about implementing or having a new national currency, the freedom to choose what to do with it. That's also the big mistake Argentina made. Repudiating 70 percent of the public debt was good. But what they didn't think about was the currency. Change the currency. Say that you can provide your economy with a new peso. Like for example, Chavez did with the new [Venezuelan] bolivar, and stop the speculation for some time in order for your own economy to stand on its feet and develop.

In the scenario you put fourth, how would you revive the economy? What would be the engine for growth? Tourism? New infrastructure?

You can have special production spheres. We need to have around 30 to 35 percent of GDP in industry and agriculture. Right now, both are less than 16 percent of the GDP. Through industry and agriculture we can have the best performance for the benefit of our economy. We can provide the people with stable employment and growing wages. We can have higher wages every year when we invest in the productivity of labor, not in the price of the labor. The two are very different. You can have a competitive economy without having to perform austerity measures against the working people.

Can the Greek industries compete globally? Also, if Greece defaults, it would not be able to trade its agricultural products with Europe because there would probably be sanctions.

Right now, more than 60 percent of the agricultural production of Greece is traded outside the European Union. We are losing every year about 5 to 10 percent from commerce inside the eurozone. So actually, right now we don't care about losing trade in the eurozone.

The motivation and the main force of our economic proposal is to improve the wages of the working people. If they have enough money, they can buy what they want and provide for the development of the economy. At the same time, the economy will provide them with more leisure time through the development of productivity. By giving leisure time, people can get involved in political activism and get involved in running the country.

Do you think that there will be a popular uprising in June or July?

We are working on a particular side of action, that's all I can say.

No one knows the future, but with the way things are going now, what do you see developing this year?

Either we will lose our statehood and become the first state under international law and in the international community that gave up its statehood, or a revolution. No middle ground.

Would you say that capitalism is in crisis globally and that it may have a few more decades to go, perhaps even less, or would you say that what we are seeing around the world are local problems?

No. It's a world situation. We have what economists call the absolute surplus of capital that cannot go into the economy so they are searching in a destructive mode to provide for more profit. And that's why the whole system is becoming more barbaric. What we have today is a capitalistic feudalism, and instead of the old lord, we have the lord of money, the banker.

We are seeing more and more Western democracies turning into police states in various places.

Not even a police state, because a police state needs to be first of all a state, an organized state. That is the opposite of what the capitalist elite want. If you have an organized country, it's bad for them, because they cannot take over easily. So they want to destroy the state and its sovereignty.

But it seems that the world is definitely moving in that direction of barbarism and feudalism you describe, so is there any way to fight that?

The Greek people have to make the first move. And that is to decide to fight for their own country. And of course, you start from the basics. The global system denies even the natural rights of the French Enlightenment. We do not see bourgeois forces fighting alongside the people, because the middle class actually is dissolving under the regime of the bankers.

"The best solidarity one can have with the Greek people is to fight against your own government." Now people can have a new type of state based on democracy that all the philosophers discussed. It's something that is quite practical and it's something that can be implemented in a record time, because of the technology and the possibilities of communication we have. That's why the most important action to take now is to fight for national sovereignty and democracy.

What's the role of international solidarity in the case of Greece? Does it even make a difference?

The best solidarity one can have with the Greek people is to fight against your own government. Because every time we have a popular movement gaining something against the global system and the local oligarchy, it's a very big help even for the Greek people. Then the average Greek citizen can say, "If they can do it, I can do it too and even better."

The only growth area in Greeces EZ economy

The Greek DEBT is paid (in other words Written Off)

"Everybody realises that Greece cannot repay its debts" Soros said last week in an interview in Spiegel. "No" says the government, the "debt is viable" we will pay it. But only this give us an extension until… 2064!

As they told us how far the fairytale goes let us summarise: Apparently everything that is being suffered by the Greek people so as to reduce the debt we are in reality experiencing the following:

In 2009 the public debt was 129% of GDP, but in 2014 (in accordance with the budget) after four years of ceaseless barbarity, after two MoU, after endless laws and measures of brigandry, after taxes, thefts and 'haircuts' the debt is to explode to 177.5% of GDP.

In other words 50 points more as a percentage of GDP than when they allegedly started to reduce it!

Πίνακας 3.1 Σύνθεση δημόσιου χρέους
(σε εκατ. ευρώ)

	2009	2010	2011	2012	2013*	2014**
Ομόλογα	272.011	276.302	259.774	86.297	76.280	59.610
Βραχυπρόθεσμοι τίτλοι	10.946	9.442	15.059	18.357	14.950	14.950
Δάνεια	15.567	54.542	93.145	200.883	234.670	250.440
Α. Χρέος Κεντρικής Διοίκησης	298.524	340.286	367.978	305.537	325.900	325.000
(ως % του ΑΕΠ)	129.2%	153.2%	176.5%	157.7%	178.2%	177.5%
Β. Χρέος ΝΠΔΔ, κέρματα κ.λπ. μείον επιχύσεις σε τίτλους ΕΔ	24.688	13.553	9.928	5.843	3.600	3.200
Γ. Χρέος Κεντρικής Κυβέρνησης κατά ESA (Α+Β)	323.212	353.839	377.906	311.380	329.500	328.200
(ως % του ΑΕΠ)	139.9%	159.3%	181.2%	160.7%	180.1%	179.3%
Δ. Χρέος ΟΤΑ, ΟΚΑ μείον ενδοκυβερνητικό χρέος	-23.522	-24.325	-22.765	-7.455	-8.500	-8.600
Ε. Χρέος Γενικής Κυβέρνησης (Γ+Δ)	299.690	329.514	355.141	303.925	321.000	319.400
(ως % του ΑΕΠ)	129.7%	148.3%	170.3%	156.9%	175.5%	174.9%
ΑΕΠ	231.081	222.151	208.532	193.749	182.911	183.089

* Εκτιμήσεις. Υπολογίστηκε ότι μέχρι 31/12/2013 θα εκταμιευτεί το σύνολο του υπολοίπου ποσού που έχει προβλεφθεί για το 2013, ύψους 4,9 δισ. ευρώ (EFSF 3,1 δισ. ευρώ και ΔΝΤ 1,8 δισ. ευρώ). Εφόσον δεν εκταμιευθεί το σύνολο του ποσού αυτού η διαφορά του θα μειώσει ισόποσα το ύψος του δημόσιου χρέους.

** Προβλέψεις

Chart showing the debt after four years of the MoU and the Troika

This downward spiral is not about to stop. It won't be stopped by the Memorandums. The Memorandums and the Troika don't reduce the debt. They never had this aim. They 'feed' the debt.

The govt's allege they take out loans (create MoU) as the country has debts. Lies! The plutocracy gets the loans. The always increasing loans are burdened on the people.

This isn't a Greek peculiarity as according to Stiglitz via this process, **the indebted countries gave to their creditors for the repayment of older debts in the period between 1984-2000 the astromomic amount of $4.6trillion**

Characteristic example which comes from the 1980's decade and is shown by accounts from the World Bank: In the beginning of 1980 the debt which 109 "indebted" countries had was $430billion dollars. Despite the fact that until 1986 they had paid interest of $336billion dollars at the end of the same year and they had ended up owing more than $880billion. **During a six year period they owed a number double what they had originally borrowed, whilst at the same time they had paid back in interest 4/5 of the original debt.**

As such, in every previous accounting of debts we had "interest collecting mechanisms which were paid over and over at least 20 times"

Εξέλιξη χρέους στην Ευρωζώνη ως ποσοστό του ΑΕΠ (%)				
Χώρα	2009	2010	2011	2012
Βέλγιο	95,7	95,7	98	99,8
Γερμανία	74,5	82,5	80	81
Ιρλανδία	64,4	91,2	104,1	117,4
Ελλάδα	129,7	148,3	170,3	156,9
Ισπανία	54	61,7	70,5	86
Γαλλία	79,2	82,4	85,8	90,2
Ιταλία	116,4	119,3	120,7	127
Κύπρος	58,5	61,3	71,5	86,6
Λουξεμβούργο	15,5	19,5	18,7	21,7
Ολλανδία	60,8	63,4	65,7	71,3
Αυστρία	69,2	72,3	72,8	74
Πορτογαλία	83,7	94	108,2	124,1
Φινλανδία	43,5	48,7	49,2	53,6
Εσθονία	7,1	6,7	6,1	9,8
Μάλτα	66,5	66,8	69,5	71,3
Σλοβακία	35,6	41	43,4	52,4
Σλοβενία	35,2	38,7	47,1	54,4
Ευρωζώνη	80	85,4	87,3	90,6
ΕΕ - 28	74,3	79,8	82,3	85,1

Development of Debt in the Eurozone as a % of GDP

As shown by yesterday's Eurostat report, the politics of the reduction of the debt has led to an increase in the debt of all the states, members of the Eurozone.

The politics of austerity, with MoU and Troikas or without, utilises the debt as an excuse for new reductions in wages, for new reductions in pensions, for new increases in taxes, for a general sellout, for the abolition of every understanding of workers rights. Continuing (with or without MoU) the same politics, the politics of the MoU, they don't minimise the debt. **They increase it, they multiply it.**

The above aren't a result of some 'mistake'. In the case of Greece there has been no 'mistake'…

The debts and deficits (or the surpluses) are part of the public wealth which is produced by the sweat of many. They are, in other words, part of the complete public wealth which a selected few take constantly. The loans which provoke the debts (they never went) to wages and pensions of workers, as ridiculously asserted "that we all ate together". They return almost in totality to the creditors and usurors! They never go (they never went) to Health and Education. They go to the banksters, the shipowners and the capitalists who use it for their businesses and **recapitalisations.** The loans never went to the non existent Welfare State. They go to cover the gaping holes of tax avoidance, tax breaks, subsidies towards the oligarchy. They are going for a massive party which is otherwise known as the Olympiad, otherwise known as submarines which permanently bend and is constantly known as NATOist armaments.

The over indebtedness constitutes (usual for capitalism) tactic of the oligarchy via which capital secures sources for its own liquidity, and consequently continues to add its own borrowings on the people.

That's where the loans went. That's where they originate from. That is what the Greek people pay.
They pay for it indefinitely.

Πίνακας 4.6 Δαπάνες εξυπηρέτησης χρέους Κεντρικής Διοίκησης (σε εκατ. ευρώ)	
Έτος	Χρεολύσια + Τόκοι κ.λπ.
1992	10.600
1993	11.070
1994	16.342
1995	17.312
1996	20.243
1997	19.262
1998	18.870
1999	18.642
2000	22.688
2001	20.946
2002	28.874
2003	30.041
2004	27.799
2005	30.066
2006	26.086
2007	31.923
2008	37.452
2009	41.460
2010	32.772
2011	45.195
2012	25.160
	Γενικό Σύνολο : 532.803

Πίνακας 4.7 Εξοφλήσεις βραχυπρόθεσμων τίτλων (σε εκατ. ευρώ)	
Έτος	Έντοκα + Βραχυπρόθεσμοι τίτλοι (σε εκατ. ευρώ)
2005	5.085
2006	8.091
2007	24.723
2008	25.674
2009	36.904
2010	22.601
2011	33.395
2012	43.607
2013	40.000
	Σύνολο : 240.080

The above facts and relative graphs which show the costs and the imposition of interest, for the maturity of bonds debts etc were in the budget of 2013 (page 133)

Proof:
1.   From Maastricht onwards, in other words in the last 20 years, the Greek people has paid to domestic and foreign usurers and profiteers the astronomic amount of E772.9b
2.   Only in 2000 and forward after the entrance of Greece into the Eurozone the Greek people had paid interest for long term loans the amazing amount of E400 billion. In the same period for the maturity debt interest of bonds we have paid E240b. **In total E640billion**
On the one hand, the state and governments are borrowing astronomic amounts with which the activity of the capitalists is secured. On the other side the people are paying for the activity of the capitalists and the state over and over again. With interest!

It is clear what is happening:
The Greek people so as to make 'viable the debt' a debt which was provoked and 'eaten' by others have paid in the last 20 years interest in the region around One Trillion Euros and now for the viability of the debt must live without wages and pensions, without work, without rights so until 2020 will have paid the same as much. Even when this is paid – in 2020 – they will 'owe' even more (if the scenario of Mr Stournaras for a 50 year bond) will be paying this until 2064. Then they will tell him they owe that much more.

Therefore from the previous if something originates as a debt from the people is the following:
The actual 'debt' of the people is identical with its existence, to be organised to resist and write off the debt which has been paid not only twice but thrice and they ask for it to be paid by our children and our grandchildren and that this already paid debt will never finish!

If something originates as a political conclusion is that this endless horror will never cease with an extension of the debt nor with haircuts nor with accounting tricks as to which is the good and which is the bad debt, which is odious and which not. The whole of the debt is odious and primarily it is already PAID. From a peoples that didn't benefit but paid it!

It's up to the people therefore to impose the political decisions which will ensure the paid debt is written off.

Postscript:
If our view is 'dogmatic' we will then quote a paragraph from an article (of the non-dogmatic) 'Kathimerini' of the last Sunday:
"Two famous economists who were associated in particular with the crisis in the Eurozone, the Belgian professor of the LSE Paul De Grawe and the Chinese lecturer of the University College of London Ms Yuemei Ji in a joint work, studied the facts and ended with this conclusion:

"An inheritance of poverty will be the non-viability of debts (...) Amongst the cases which they use to defend their conclusion is Italy Portugal Spain and naturally as you have understood our country. If we assume that Greece pays interest not greater that the rhythm of annual economic growth for the debt to be reduced to 90% of GDP they will require between 22 to 50 years depending on the annual budget surpluses. They will require 50 years for the budget surplus to be 2% annually, for 30 years for it to be 3% and for 22 years for it to be 4%. This will mean the imposition of extreme austerity for 22 years or heavy austerity for 30 years (but nevertheless austerity) or less extreme austerity for half a century for 50 years…"

Nikos Bogiopoulos

What Greece Produces?
Research study by PASEGES (Agricultural Coops Union)

For many months a wide range of the political system and sections of the Left, distribute and circulate ridiculous terror of fear regarding the alleged destructive consequences which an exit of Greece would have from the Euro. These scenarios have reached the stage of pretending that we would have mass hunger and the emergence of cannibalism, due to the lack of surely in basic agricultural goods. But according to the President of the National Federation of Farmers Coperatives (PASEGES) , Tasks to Karemiha "even if we go to the Drachma, Greeks won't go hungry as autarky in the country of basic agricultural products reaches ...94%

1) Magnesium Greece produces 46% of the total production of the EU

2) Aluminium a few years ago France reduced its production and Greece is number one in Europe

3) Bauxite
Greece is the largest producer in the EU and this is used in the construction of airplanes, electrical appliances and metallic constructions and others

4) Smektites

Greece is the 2nd country in the world after the USA with the extract of smektites they have a wide range of use in medicines, perfumes, etc.

5) Nickel

Greece is the only country in the EU with serious deposits of nickel in its grounds. It has a production facility for nickel the biggest in the European Union, but is mostly exported alongside everything that is extracted.

6) Olive Oil

We are the 3rd largest producer of olives and oil. That's what God gave us, but we continue to buy industrial deal and then get ill.
We have 15% of world production (olive-oil)

7) Saffron

We are the 3rd country of production of saffron Kozanis.

8. Asparagus

We are the 5th country on earth in the production of asparagus

9) Cotton

We are the 7th country in the export of cotton. In 2004 we were 4th We are the 11th in the production of cotton.

10) Tourism

We are 14th in the arrival of tourists (18m)

11) Cheese

We are 16th in the export of cheese products

12) Shipping
Num 1 on the planet

The above were stated by Mr Karamiha in the last executive meeting of PASEGES in Thessaloniki, in an attempt to show the dynamism and the possibilities of the Greek agricultural economy. An agricultural economy that shows that it continues to exist despite the constant attacks by CAP (Common Agricultural Policy), of the EU and its warped many times subsidised.

The facts of PASEGES which were presented in relation to agricultural autarky in relation to the relevant study of PASEGES which was presented on Wednesday, the % of autarky in a series of basic agricultural edible products of vegetable and animal production were around 94% in 2010.

In vegetable production we have around 99% surely, on average not in every product, like pulses where we have 82% surely the lowest amount being, wheat 32% and the highest rice (171%)
In fruits as have the biggest autarchy in oranges (167%) whilst in lemons this is limited to 67%.
In fruits in general autarky remains high around 128% whilst its low in pulses. (39%)
In animal production its around 73%

In meat its around 56% in Fitzroy whilst the smallest percentage of beef is 30% but for sheep and goat meet around 94%
In cheeses yoghurts autarky etc is around 80% sugary whilst for feta cheese its is 147% autarky.

In honey and eggs we have around 92% and 91% autarky
Developments in agricultural economy leads to a
significant fall in production of the agricultural sector of
Greece which is quite intense during 2006-11 particularly
great during 2006 - leading to a 14% fall and also a 4% fall
during 2008-9. During the two year period 2010-11 there
was a limited increase not more than 2%.
Of particular intensity is the fall of plant production during
2005-11 which is associated with the fall of prices of
production. Based on estimations of the European statistics
service, the value of plant production was limited to €6.9b
from €8.2b in 2006, a 16% drop.
With respect to bank financing of the agricultural sector
we see that only 1.7% of total bank lending goes to
agriculture.

The wages of the agricultural sector have been In a
downward spiral since 2008.

During the 2006-2011 period farmers income as shown by
Eurostat was reduced by 22.6% whilst in the same period
farmers income in Greece was increased by 19% and the
countries of the eurozone by about 5%

Κρίσιμη παράμετρος της πτώσης του αγροτικού
εισοδήματος παραμένει η σημαντική αύξηση του κόστους
παραγωγής, με το μέσο γενικό δείκτη εισροών, σύμφωνα
με τα στοιχεία της στατιστικής υπηρεσίας, να καταγράφει
νέα σημαντική αύξηση, της τάξεως των 7,5 ποσοστιαίων
μονάδων, προερχόμενη κυρίως από τη σημαντική αύξηση
στους δείκτες της ενέργειας (17,1%), των ζωοτροφών
(11,9%) και των λιπασμάτων (10,7%).

Critical measure of the collapse of farmers income has been the significant increase in the costs of production due to the increases in the price of energy (17%), animal feeds (12%) and fertiliser (10%))

www.patari .org

D. Mass immigration NWO tool of the 4th Reich

Introduction

One needs to go back 25 years to recall what was written about mass immigration into Greece by a joint parliamentary committee encompassing all the main political parties including the Left. A section of the document is enclosed. Suffice to say Greece never had colonies in the modern capitalist era and as such did not control vast tracts of land in what is known as the third world.

The mass influx of people into Greece since the fall of the Soviet Union led to serious problems both of integration, assimilation and economic survival. Slowly but surely Greeks were replaced from all manual trades and those that didn't go abroad were taken over by the new influx of people both from E Europe as from Asia.

This is a taboo topic by the majority of the fake Left as they believe in the EU Empire, they have fundamental agreements with globalization and as has been seen inthe few months in power of Syriza, hundreds of thousands are arriving after they opened the borders with Turkey and de facto abolished Dublin 2.

When S Samoilis MP came over as a representative of Syriza from Corfu and spoke in the British Parliament he was specifically asked by the Labour Partys health spokeseperson Dianne Abbot no questions on Health but how Greece is treating its black and asian immigrants. As a representative of her Majestys Opposition Abbot was only concerned to prove the charge of 'racism', such is the level of politics from the imperialist heartlands that those who had the larges land empire in history view all countries with socio economic problems as not doing everything to bend their back to the multitudes that decide at any moment in time to venture towards Greece as its in the Euro and the currency is traded with the whole planet. Samoilis MP tried a mealy mouthed defence by stating the country can't essentially cope, but Syriza will do its hardest to have humane treatment.

After six months in power the 'humane' treatment of hundreds of thousands arriving was closing down all immigration reception centres, (set up in 2012 as a consequence of Greeks rioting) allowing anyone and everyone to destroy island ports and tourism and build portacabins to house... 170. Syriza was unilaterally going to abolish Dublin 2 regulations, they were going to solve the immigration issue as opposed to what went on before, which was a free for all. As usual its practice that counts not words. Syriza allowed an even bigger free for all, refused to call in the UN and declare a state of emergency on the islands some of which have seen 10 times more illegal immigrants arriving than citizens.

Glezos gave an interview on the issue which has been buried by the Syriza tops as globalism trumps any other response.

There have been reports as to the true nature of the 4th Reich by the UN Population Division reports. They argue that due to the ageing of Europe's population it has to double in the next period of 50 years to maintain pensions, when in reality they want no pensions Chinese style, work to be 16hours, and the absolute privatization of all health care. It's a 4th Reich where Brussels decide all economic and social policy ignoring the wishes of the Greek Parliament and social dumping becomes a generalized rule. Of course the mass media of corporate power sell these events as aiding refugees, saving the destitute the world over and providing to the poor as they have saved Greece from destruction. It's the old Vietnam trick destroying the village in order to ...save it.

A return to a national currency would also have a big impact in relation to the mass immigration inflows. Few would want to come to Greece if it had the drachma as capital controls would be in place, it would not be a hard currency and the export of it would be complicated unlike the Euro. Another reason why the political establishment which is beholden to the shipowners of Greece does not want a break with the Euro. They see mass immigration as a tool to break all wage/conditions demands as a massive oversupply of labour cannot sustain any pressure against the boss class.

This does not imply that there are no refugees or that every individual is a war refugee as is currently being touted by the corporate mass media and foreign presstitutes like Paul Mason (who sells globalism adopting every immigrant who sets foot in Greece) and who also was instrumental in selling Syriza's 'left face' during the so called negotiations with the Troika.

The Greek bosses fully opened the borders with Albania back in the early 1990's and effectively made the Greek labour movement redundant with an oversupply of labour. Now Greeks in manufacturing or agriculature represent less that 15% of the actual labour force and as such the social composition of political parties of the Left are such that they are mostly middle class and as they crisis gets worse the middle class moves further and further to the right accepting and promoting every agenda of the bosses however it is sold and the latest being humanitarianism in the service of illegal immigration, which replaced 'humanitarian interventions' like in ex Yugoslavia.

There is now a hyperglobalist degenerate tendency which argues: 'Let them All In...' ie Open Borders in the here and now.

How else could big business sell the mass movement of peoples from Asia Africa and Latin America to the USA-EU?

Refugees are a selling point. There are wars in many places. Refugees are created. Most manufacturing business has moved to Asia. Now the aim is to move Asia and Africa to Europe.

Cutting labour costs is all the rage. The problems will always remain. Lowering European wages to Asian and African levels won't sell more imported goods. It will collapse trade... Without union controls in labour supply, real refugees not economic migrants globalism dominates and what was achieved in terms of labour conditions will be leveled out the world over.

Cross Party Parliamentary Committee on Mass Immigration into Greece

The Left knew there would be a massive problem in Greece they are co-signatories to this Parliamentary Committee (1993) both Syrizas predecessors Sinaspismos and the KKE. They didn't integrate or unionise the first thousands of illegals that arrived. They allowed through their leadership in unions for the situation to spiral out of control. We have now had riots in two major cities untold citizens committees being created on the issue and they are concerned alongside the Troika only about Golden Dawn, the retro fascist fake nationalists in order to give themselves a boost. When an indigenous working class is overrun by a similar number of illegals then a national question re-emerges. How one deals with this and what will happen next we leave to history. Suffice to say when Greeks are being killed on average 5 a month by illegals it wont be peaceful...

VN Gelis

GREEK PARLIAMENT
Crossparty Parliamentary Committee
For the study of the demographic problem of the country

and the presentation of proposals for their more serious confrontation.

CONCLUSION

Chairman Vasileos Sotiropoulos Argolida MP New Democracy
Vice President Vasileos Geratidisi Thessaloniki B' Constitutency PASOK
Secretary Manolis Drettakis A' Dsitrict Athens MP, Sinaspismos

Athens
February 1993
The demographic Problem of Greece and the proposals for confronting it

Page 1
In our country which has one of the lowest birth rates the demographic problems takes important national characteristics which may *threaten our national independence and territorial integrity*

Page 2
In the National Committee we also discusees two further questions of Manolis Drettakis (12/279 and 14/2/86) plus proposal of laws of MP's of PASOK 'motivations for the confrontation of the demographic problem of the country' on 7th and 28th November 1991.

Committee Members
1. Σωρηρόπουλος Βασίλειος
2. Ανδρακτάς Παναγιώτης
3. Βαρδαρινός Βασίλειος
4. Γεωργολιός Κωνσταντίνος
5. Κανελλοπούλου Κρινιώ
6. Καραγκούνης Ανδρέας
7. Μπακογιάννη Ντόρα
8. Πάλλη Πετραλιά Φάνη
9. Παπαγεωργόπουλος Ελευθέριος
10. Παπανικολάου Ελευθέριος
11. Τατούλης Πέτρος
12. Χωματάς Ιωάννης
13. Γερανίδης Βασίλειος
14. Κρητικός Παναγιώτης
15. Κωνσταντινίδης Ελευθέριος
16. Μπαλτάς Αλέξανδρος
17. Παπαδόπουλους Βασίλειος
18. Παπαθεμελής Στυλιανός
19. Πάχτας Χρήστος
20. Σμπώκος Ιωάννης
21. Δρεττάκης Μανόλης (EAP) Sinaspismos
22. Κοσιώνης Παναγιώτης (KKE)

The members of the Committee Andreas Bakoyianni Dora,
Palli Petralia Fani were replaced later, due to them
undertaking ministerial duties from the MP's Theodoro
Georgiadis, Dimopoulos Demetrios and Theodoro Katsiki
whilst the position of the recently deceased in July 1992
Papadopoulos Vasiliou was received by the MP Skoulakis
Emmanuel.

Pg 15

The repatriation of political refugees and the mass arrival of compatriots (Pontion and Northern Ipirus) with a correct political intervention will have positive results. The state should help them base themselves and work, not only in the city centres but also in the agricultural and semi-agricultural areas and to provide a new dynamic to many agricultural areas primarily in Northern Greece. The common cultural roots and Orthodoxy would help them adapt and assimilate into Greek society.

Particular attention should be placed by the entrance and employment of tens of thousands of foreign immigrants legal (but mostly illegal) arrive in our country in the two last decades. Whilst the percentage of unemployment is around 8% in many sectors there is a lack of labour hands which has been covered primarily by foreign illegal immigrants.

With the illegal arrival of immigrants – mostly muslims from Afro-asian countries, Greece is being transformed into an area of receiving immigrants which creates social economic problems (conflicts in the labour market, increase in tax evasion with many consequences in the national insurance coffers, an increase in criminality, movement of drugs etc.) and they can't adapt to Greek society due to the totally different culture of Islam, which isn't simply a religion, but a way of life

Page 24
-The distance from the traditional forms of life and the arrival of events of social decay with the undermining of the principles of marriage, family life and children have a significant influence on the demographic issues.
-The highest form of individualism, the weakening of morality, drugs, AIDS and generally the social undermining and the world insecurity influence negatively the demographic problem.
-Future population development of Greece

Page 27
If the demographic indicators aren't improved and the same indicators of birth in 1990 (1.4 roughly average children per woman) and if they don't develop significant events (war, immigration) then the total population of the country in 2015 will be reduced by 500,000 people from today's numbers. The increase in these demographic indicators which started in 1985 creates severe problems of population in our country. The empty spaces which are created cover by a larger part from Pontius and Northern Epirus but also from Muslims from Asia and Africa and from others who illegally enter Greece (and remain with a variety of fake conditions adding new problems)

Social economic factors which influence the demographic problem

Demographic consequences

Page 30
Our country with the dramatic reduction of births in the last decade has the possibility of big dangers (which are being intensified due to the geographical position and the lack of cooperative peoples);
-The reduction of births in the 1980's decade whereby the indicators fell from 2.09 children per woman to 1.4 in 1990, threatens quite severely the re-birth and continuation of our Greek race.

-The demographic gaps which are created in various geographic areas (Aegean islands, Ionian etc) have as the danger to be occupied by immigrants (mostly Muslims) with severe endless consequences.
-In the armed forces we will create serious problems with the lack of numbers of those in the armed forces.

Page 31
If for the re-birth of our labour dynamic and generally the course of our economy and our social security we are based on the immigrants from Asia and Africa very soon we will have serious problems of social and national

Aims of Greek Demographic Politics - Proposals

Page 36
-To emphasise at every available moment Greek tradition and religious feeling (practically with proposals of the Church)

Administrative measures

Page 40
-The illegal and easy entrance of illegal immigrants from countries of Asia and Africa either directly or via other countries of the EU must be observed closely for many social economic and national reasons. There must be severe control regarding the legality of the entrance in our country and the legal presence and employment.

Ghettoes in central Athens

Athens 10th February 1993

Greek Riots over Illegal Immigration

What started off as small protests in central Athens (6th District around Agios Panteleomonas) by concerned citizens regarding the massive rise in illegal immigration has now spread to other areas of Greece with the 'pre-electoral' announcement of Hrisohoidis-Interior Minister that 30 illegal Immigration Reception centres will be built all over Greece to house the officially arriving 300 a day from the non-existent borders of Greece.

This situation, 20 years in the making, has turned central Athens into a 'third world' reception centre with no infrastructure to cope with the mass influx. Not having colonies in the modern era of the rise of capitalism Greece neither has the schools, hospitals or the capacity to cope. Daily Greeks are robbed, killed or maimed in violent looting sprees which resemble the conditions of banana republics of central America, (according to reports 1,400 Greeks have been murdered in the last 12 years by illegal immigrants) and Hrisohoidis pronouncements that he will 'clean up the centre' and tackle illegal immigration, are just pronouncements added on to previous ones, the arrival of Frontex or the building of a wall in Evros. All show and no content, the stark reality is that Europe's porous borders (latest figures show that 68% of new arrivals come in via Greece) is a long term imperialist strategy for the promotion of cheap labour and the replacement of indigenous labour with globalised labour.

No one in Greece believes the governments any more on anything. Hence the reaction has been rioting in a series of areas against these so-called reception centres (essentially holding pens to spread round illegal immigrants as the centre of Athens can no longer hold). The fake Left, proponents of mass illegal immigration two decades now (KKE famously refused to unionise Albanian building workers instead becoming sub-contractors to this labour and their politics reflected this change) alongside the globalists of Syriza suddenly remembered this is a problem. Yet not once have they had a single demonstration in relation to this issue, not once have they protested about Greeks being murdered. As if in tandem they have left the door open to the 'far right' retro fascists of Golden Dawn and from the sidelines have criticised Greeks who protest as being ....fascist. Yet who agreed to the foreign occupation of Greeks by a multitude of arrivals? The Greeks certainly didn't and now there have been at least 5 large riots over the issue in a variety of areas where these alleged 'new reception areas are to be built. No wonder that in electoral polls the vote for the retro fascists hovers between 10-20% in certain central electoral districts.

One of the slogans of the participants is that the 'whole of Greece will be like Keratea'....where the PASOK government was defeated over its attempts to turn an area into a large rubbish dump without taking into account the wishes of the local people, and where Pangalos (the then Vice President) declared that PASOK lost the struggle on behalf of the Troika, in Keratea.

The irony on the whole situation is that there are still globalists who believe the Greek capitalist class is against illegal immigration and cheap labour at the same time as one of the reasons the Greek Seafarers Association is on strike is the abolition of indigenous crews (cabotage as it is known) in line with the previous abolition of Greek crews that happened in Greek shipping more than 3 decades ago.

Daily arrivals of more than 300 just in the Evros region
http://farofylakes.blogspot.co.uk/2012/04/blog-post_1847.html

The Left covers the illegal low lifes

http://en.wikipedia.org/wiki/Manolis_Glezos

Interview with Manolis Kotakis
Newspaper 'Democracy'

Q: Dear Glezos, Athens is in turmoil after the murder by immigrants of Manolis Kantaris. The Left just as like in the pre-war era and the rise of fascism, doesn't seem to be expressing the citizens with what it stands for and they are looking towards the Far Right. What is at fault?

Glezos: This is a big problem. The situation in many suburbs is unacceptable. The people cannot live by being confronted by all this wave which exploits immigrants. The mafias of immigrants, the low lifes made up of immigrants, I do not shirk from saying it, are creating problems for the citizens.

Who is at fault for this? Let us see the root of the evil. All the European governments are at fault, in particular those which had colonies in today's under development countries (Africa Asia) which ceased to be colonial but continue to exploit these countries and don't allow them to develop. The cause are the ex-colonialists. The govt is also at fault as its subordinate to the demands of Dublin 2 and does not do what it must. They should get everyone ask them where are you from and if they answered for example from Algeria send him packing to France! Get France to pay for this cause. They should have provided them with the right documents and send them to the colonial countries. Thirdly why should only the citizens of Ag Panteleomonas and Kipseli pay for this (immigration influx translators edit) and not Psihiko and Filothei (rich suburbs translators edit)? Another issue. The govt uses the police as an organ of oppression of social struggles, instead of an organ for the suppression of criminality. If it acted out the latter we wouldn't have so many crimes. They would be avoided.

Q: And the Left?

Glezos: What I say it doesn't repeat! The Left takes uncritically the side of the immigrants without condemning the criminal mafias, who act amongst the immigrants and does not distinguish the issue. From there onwards is the ground on which fascism develops. I am questioning then. Where was the Left at fault to not be able to stop the rise of fascism in the pre-war era? The question is as valid today!

16th May 2012

E. Debates with NWO pseudo leftists on Greece

Anglo American Globalists vs IMFvsGreece blogspot

David Walters(Marxist Internet Archive): An American Provocateur Proponent of the NWO and One World Government

> "Dear comrades, if we shall keep mum today, tomorrow the Jewish Marxists will ride on our backs... Vladimir Lenin"

"The Greek people are anarchic and difficult to tame. For this reason we must strike deep into their cultural roots: Perhaps then we can force them to conform. I mean, of course, to strike at their language, their religion, their cultural and historical reserves, so that we can neutralize their ability to develop, to distinguish themselves, or to prevail; thereby removing them as an obstacle to our strategically vital plans in the Balkans, the Mediterranean, and the Middle East."
(As reported in the popular Greek magazine, Oikonomikos Tachydromos on 14 Aug. 1997, Henry Kissinger, while addressing a group of Washington, D.C. businessmen in Sept.1974)

"They condemn us that we want to abolish borders and dissolve the State. But the State we build today no longer exists as they dissolved it. Who therefore is a

patriot? They or us? Capital doesn't have a country and it runs to find profit in whatever country it is able to. That is why it isn't concerned for the existence of borders and the state. But all we own are our hats and the small kerb in front of us, unlike capital that runs wherever it finds profit."
Aris Velouhiotis- Partisan Leader of Greece 1944

http://www.marxists.org/archive/velouchiotis/1945/x01/x01.htm
A section of the article that Walters refused to upload on MIA and only after consistent complaints do they appear.

Show me who your friends are….
On who runs MIA and their piece in the New York Times (House Organ of US Imperialism) plus the dubious role of a Brian Bagsen (an avowed anti-bolshevik in charge of the Russian section!!)
"Historical Bias: I believe Marxism was a complete failure as a form of government. Hence, it follows that I believe that Marxism has been a failure when in the form of a political party. Yet, despite these failures, it has an ever present connection to radical mass movements, which is an interesting paradox. I openly loathe Bolshevism and vanguardism, which I firmly believe leads to horribly unethical government where the ends justify the means. Needless to say, these beliefs often put me at odds with many in this organization, and eventually led to my depature."
Brian Bagsen's Biography

"I wish we had MORE of him…"
David Walters

At the end of the 90's David Walters flew to Greece like others before him, to use their skills in setting up some new venture that which later became the Marxist Internet Archive. I was informed of him and asked to try and make contact. At the time of the NATO bombardment of Serbia egged on by British imperialism with mass protests in Greece (where nooses were set up for Tony Blair and the weekly satirical magazines 'Pontiki' had him in a gay pose with Clinton) this must have affected the American for over the next decade and a half he has engaged in an internet stalking relationship on behalf of American imperialism against myself. I came across him over the debates regarding Seattle where another American group (Spartacist League) condemned the protests and called them reactionary and nationalist as workers complained against Chinese imports and abstained from them.

Visit to the USA
Walters was involved in disrupting a visit to a now disbanded self-proclaimed Marxist Workers Group in Detroit over the fact that I reprinted what Engels wrote on homosexuality and the fact that the leader of this group said in late 1999 that there was no 'immigration' problem to Greece and there was no 'open border policy of US-EU imperialism in place'. We arrived at Detroit international airport and waited and waited for them. They turned up to tell us that something had happened which they didn't explain and after a day we left as we were provided with nowhere to sleep and left to fend for ourselves having to leave at 6am to get out of the city. On arriving at a

McDonalds we were told to move away as we were the wrong colour and could end up dead before we could find a taxi.

9/11 Fake Terror and anti-Iranian venom

Over the course of a decade Walters has trumpeted vociferously the 9/11 put up job which launched the 'war on terror' and bankrupted the USA. He alleges that he has connections with a French group though no one ever has verified it and according to himself he is a loner. I would classify him as an American deadbeat who lives in a Potemkin village world of make believe. In the same period the same friend who helped set up the Marxist Internet Archive noticed that a whole host of anti-communist stuff was appearing and some of the editors on the threads were avowed and self-declared anti-Bolsheviks and this was noted in a circular sent out by me to many US organisations as they refused to upload translations done by myself either from English to Greek or from Greek to English from Greece's revolutionary historical past. They kept on citing various problems when it came to Greek translations from computer malfunctions to html codes etc. They also refused to upload material on the Greek civil war written by Greeks so we were forced to produce a book on it...

At the same time he kept on stating our views are marginal in Greece (five or so ex-organisations that make up the collective Patriotic Left) that Greece is a sub-imperialist country and they can receive an unlimited number of illegal immigrants as the EU has deemed this necessary via the Dublin 2 agreement, that no one has published any study on Marxism and Immigration (D Dousias in 2009 who presided over the only scientific analysis of the Greek Roma and who has been included in my latest work on Immigration http://imfoccupationgreece.blogspot.com/) and he appears to support all Americans who voice **the opinion that Greeks as a nation should be overrun erased etc and become like the USA** (which is the starting point of all conversations ie how wonderful is the 'multicultural' ghetto of the USA and its export should be a sine non qua for the labour movement everywhere and anywhere). John Reinman on the self-styled 'socialist' discussion group voiced the same opinion from Oakland California that it has been overrun by all and sundry and that this is essentially wonderful. So the Yank experience becomes the world experience and if one doesn't subscribe to that schema one is labelled ...racist. This coming from a country that called Vietnamese 'gooks', Arabs 'sand niggers' and kept blacks segregated up till 1970 and just as they stopped segregation they got them all to join the prison industrial complex having a higher incarceration rate than anywhere else on earth etc. Its as if we now all live in the international departure of an airport lounge and we shake hands with everyone we meet say 'gia sou' and this is now called 'international socialism' not globalism of the most rotten kind. Whoever uses Oakland California as a starting point in anything needs their head examined. That's where we don't want to end up.

Walters then goes on to berate a member of the Patriotic Left for being in Tehran when the main topic was 9/11 and how WW2 was used to justify the creation of the state of Israel. These views (bar the Anglo-American fake left) are widespread in France and Greece as an ex-central committee member of the French CP Garaudy wrote on the state of Israel a long time ago. Walters hides behind the collaborationist French govts past history to support left Zionism and label people 'anti-semitic' for they dare breach the topic of the US airbase in the Middle East. An old tired trick that no longer holds water but works well in US academia and the far left globalist circuits that label people either 'conspiracy theorists' 'holocaust deniers' ad nauseum. Having lost uncles in Hitler's concentration camps it is a bit of a cheek to argue that I believe there were no concentration-extermination camps. Why don't we just say what Walters really means. There was only one Holocaust, the jewish one and it trumps all others and anyone questioning the depth and severity of it must deny it existed for after all how can we collect money to prop up the Zionist entity if we haven't got a story to sell?

Degeneration of the US 'far left'...
In years of old before they became corrupted an American group wrote this

[O]n a sufficiently large scale, immigration flows could wipe out the national identity of recipient countries.... If, for example, therewere unlimited immigration into Northern Europe, the population influxfrom the Mediterranean basin would tend to dissolve the national identity of small countries like Holland and Belgium. More generally, unlimited immigration as a principle is incompatible with the right ofnational self-determination; to call for it is tantamount to advocating the abolition of national states under capitalism."
Workers Vanguard's original article on the subject (January 18,
1974):

Now they send me articles castigating the 'nationalism' of the Greek labour movement in other words accept your lot don't complain and don't protest. Between an armed revolution and global revolution there are a multitude of ways the issue of illegal immigration could be wrested from the fake rightists.

Most of the American 'far left' groups degenerated in the 70's into self appreciation societies which became infatuated with the individual self and adopted the policies of lifestyles (paedophilia, gay, lesbian now trans) just like the Ottoman Empire did in 1864 before its ignominious collapse and it is an irony of history that then Anglo-French imperialism considered them 'backward' for legalizing homosexuality (before the Russian Revolution) and coined a phrase in French (shagging like a Greek!) and now British imperialism is on a mission via Camerons foreign office to 'educate' the backward members of the Commonwealth and actively promote homosexual lifestyles (majority of countries which have homosexuality banned on their statute books are from the ex-Commonwealth countries)

The arrival and perpetual legalization of immigrants in the USA (11million under Obama) became the second most adopted slogan from the 'far left' groups there. Anyone raising any objections was also labelled reactionary and backward as if the destruction of historic nations (which have a history far greater than the bastard offspring of British Imperialism) is a principle that anyone other than real fascists can espouse in this day and age whereby unelected central banksters and their political offshoots dictate who lives and who dies.

We had a decade of being told we live in Fortress Europe and then we realise this was just the propaganda trick used by the globalists for a 'fortress' which has the front gate open wide ain't a fortress.

There were groups of ex-trotskyists (Vitsoris group) who during the course of the last direct imperialist occupation of Greece who claimed opposing the 3rd Reich was futile, Germany is unifying Europe, it is bringing the working class into closer unity forgetting that the abolition of nations is a decision nations should be allowed to take by themselves not imposed from above with the presence of army officers or from turning national tax offices into the vehicle of imposing bankster rules as they have done in Greece and have imposed in Cyprus (via the bailin).

Agios Panteleomonas 2008 Immigration Question goes National
When local residents started to complain and protest about the unchecked arrival and squatting of hundreds of illegal immigrants who used the square to live, sell drugs, go to the toilet harangue the local Greek girls and old women by relieving them of their gold jewellery (mostly a Christian cross) one should have said these Greeks are racist they aren't open to the world despite since the 70's having the 4th most tourists in the EU.

When predominantly women set up committees and egged on men to do something about the fact they couldn't go about their daily business, men were forced into action.

The corporate media that represents the interests of globalism started a vociferous campaign against the residents labelling them 'racists. On the back of this campaign the 'leftists' who work in tandem with the corporate media started to march and march and march against the local residents. Riot police turned up and threw tear gas into the main church. The residents stood firm beyond all the odds. Walters labelled all these residents ...nazis.

Lets now look at Walters line on immigration, its due to the root causes of imperialisms decay, the collapse of societies due to war and population movements across borders. If I am not mistaken the war in Vietnam started in 1945 and lasted till 1975 a full thirty years. The civil war in Yugoslavia and the imperialist intervention lasted another decade in the 1990's. The amount of Vietnamese or Serbs that arrived in Greece can be numbered in the palm of one hand. Now why is that? All immigration according to Walters is 'progressive' 'anti-imperialist' for we are dealing with 'immigrant rights' UN conventions and as Felicity Lawrence said 'migration theory'. Iraqui and Afghani collaborators of Western imperialism never crossed the borders into Greece chased out by those resisting imperialism in their territories only victims of ...imperialism. Collaborators become an above class entity (migrants) and they gain supra-national rights. The labour movement of each country based within specific national borders have no rights to question anyone and anything. They have to be open in order to not be 'xenophobic'.

So when we had underage girls being pimped by Nigerian drug dealers in central Athens 100m from Omonia square we have to put this down to 'migration theory' ie pimping has gone global and there is nothing to be done. Locals aren't allowed to say anything as they weren't allowed to say anything in the slums of South Africa when the same phenomena appeared. Long live the unity of international pimps and underage prostitution should be added as another one of Walters 'transitional demands' in the current era. When the Algerian resistance banned prostitution and alcohol and took out severe measures against those who flouted the rules, we should have argued they are oppressing the rights of 'sex workers' and they should be free to ply their trade with occupation troops, otherwise this shows the chauvinistic oppression by males of Algerian women?

When the corporate media journalists who are nothing more than hired whores of capitalism in decay arrive in any scene they dictate the terms of the news agenda not based on what happened and why but on what we need to say and gather facts accordingly. Paul Mason arrived in Patras interviewed a few people and declared there was a Golden Dawn riot against illegal immigrants from the offices of the BBC as always which has a monopoly of the truth (same BBC that announced half an hour before it collapsed the 3rd Tower during 9/11 and also the non-existent finding of weapons of mass destruction to justify the Iraqui invasion). Although given airtime and does circuits in Universities and book fairs as to how the working class has gone global to sell books for his much needed pension pot so he can retire in some idyllic setting.

The reality was a Greek woke up one night heard a whole bunch of noise, went out to tell some people to shut up, not knowing they were lumpen illegal hoodlums and they stabbed him to death. In the disused ex-fabric producing factory Piraiki Patraiki they went to hide. The next morning locals gathered to protest and find them. The police arrived on the scene to save them from a riot. The locals stole a road digger to attack one of the ex-factory walls. GD arrived on the scene in the form of party leaders and informed the road digger owner his road digger had been stolen trying to diffuse the situation. The police then used helicopters to ship out those inside the factory to the safety of Athens. So hundreds of residents involved in more than a few days battle with riot cops (many had to be shipped in from Athens) were labelled GD. Problem solved. Who is Paul Mason? Ex leftie leader of Workers Power. Totally impartial as always, being British helps when reporting on Greece...having a past as a colonial overlord. Mustn't let tradition get in the way of a good revisionist story after all we have agendas to sell.

Walters then castigates another poster for uploading Marx's comments on immigration rounding on him as if they were uploaded by me. This is the style of 'debate' hatchet job man who pretends he actually is listened to by anyone and rounds on them if they mention Marx on Immigration. Well here is a blogsite only with comments by Marx and Engels on Immigration. Read at your peril cos you won't find most on the MIA, they don't do that sort of thing. They are respectable with Stalin and Rorty all over.
http://classicalmarxismvsimmigration.blogspot.com/

Nuclear Power apologist...

After the ban by the now disbanded Permanent Revolution group Walters went round campaigning for nuclear power how progressive it is and how it will end 'global warming' in particular just as Fukushima occurred. Despite the facts against the topic eg Pripyat 25 years after Chernobyl is a city still evacuated of 50k citizens as the readings are 75k times higher than they were before the explosion. An American true to form everything that is rotten from the states he wants exported. He has found 'safe' nuclear power despite the fact that Pripyat is now burnt out for at least 600 years due to radioactivity, the same with Fukyshima and despite the protests in Japan that saw 200k citizens march outside the Presidential Palace, but hey lets ignore mass movements, we know better, nuclear power is safe...Walters said so and as an American one must take their hat off to him.

British 'far left' and Greece
Just like they did nothing for the struggle of independence for Kenya prior to that what is it they did regarding Britain's involvement in fostering Greece's civil war and supporting the collaborators of Hitler?
Answers on a postcard please. Prize a book of mine on the Greek civil war.
http://www.amazon.co.uk/Greek-Civil-War-VN-Gelis/dp/1468011545/ref=sr_1_1?s=books&ie=UTF8&qid=1375609286&sr=1-1&keywords=the+greek+civil+war
The British 'far left' has always been in the overwhelming majority pro-imperialist alongside their American counterparts. Their support is always based on the 'ethnics' behaving themselves and following what the centre decides.

WRP-Gerry Healy had an organisation in Greece which destroyed the first post-dictatorial printshop after expelling the majority of the organisation in a typical healyite frame up and shutting down all the bookshops. Throughout this period Bob Archer was with Gerry Healy and not only that, when their honcho in Athens (another self-styled fake jew Savvas Michael) was parading in Tehran and Libya singing the praises in order to get money from there we were supposed to keep quiet when allegations regarding rape and financial fraud were aired in public for the first time. I made a special journey to the UK to interview their Gestetner trade union rep they had called Richard Goldstein and translated the interview and with a series of reports, posters and adverts in 'Pontiki' exposed the WRP and called for a Commission of Inquiry (as to whether they had handed over pictures of Iraqui communists to Saddam and taken money from the oil-igarchs) but the successors to Healy weren't interested only in trying to maintain Healyism without... Healy. In the 90's Archers alliances with Slaughter were based on an anti-Serb venom paralleled only by Blair (who obviously had guns). There is a saying in Greek 'show me who your friends are and I will tell you who you are' fits accordingly with Bob Archer and David Walters. A marriage made in heaven.

The Militant had followers in PASOK who were in PASOK. One wing 'left' in 1991 another about three years ago. What discerned them was their slavish acceptance of PASOK as being 'social democratic' instead of pure capitalist (liberal centre party of Greek capitalism) and their careerist appetites. When things started to rock they jumped ship in order to find new homes (latest declaring themselves the 'communist wing in Syriza and supporting the Euro, EZ and EU!!) Those that joined PASOK or were allied to it did it for material gain, there wasn't much politics and there hasn't been much since. When hundreds of thousands hit the squares swearing at Parliament and the PASOK and ND MP's how did they cdes of Militant in Greece feel? Their whole lifetime in politics was geared around being in PASOK. Insofar as they marched in the 70's chanting **'US bases Out' 'National Independence and Territorial Integrity'' EC and NATO are the Same' Greece Belongs to the Greeks'** they weren't racist or nationalist, but John Reinman http://oaklandsocialist.com/ if he was a member then forgets the 'sins' of his youth and in old age seeks revenge to those who remind him of his past. Now if they weren't the slogans being chanted confirm that with those who were there...

SWP Greece has been one of the most vociferous in gaining EU subsidies to promote 'diversity and multiculturalism' through their open border Soros networks (Athens Indymedia run on govt platforms from the Athens Polytechnic), language schools for foreigners, social forums etc and it's no coincidence that when they were exposed way back in 2004 I was banned from even broaching the subject in their media. Half their organisation after the SWP UK touting it as being the biggest in Greece joined Sinaspismos to get an electoral subsidy and now in the leader of Davanelos they parade as being the 'left opposition' inside Syriza when they have been known to support every anti-Greek act by foreign US subsidised govt's eg Skopje when they marched there holding up the flags of a foreign territory which has claims on Greece, over the issue of Macedonia. When hundreds of thousands of Greeks marched in the 90's against the USA's attempts at divide and rule they resurrected the hundreds of thousands who marched during the 3rd Reich (when it handed over a section of northern Greece to Bulgaria without fear for their lives and many were killed.)

They consistently campaigned against the citizens groups that sprung up in central Athens turning up with the riot cops to tear gas them and hurl abuse from 2008 onwards. GD turned up for the same reasons to pay lip service to the struggle of the residents in order to gather votes. Now because the SWP are the marketing agents for GD (they both call each other Bolsheviks and nazi respectively when they are nothing of the sort just two sides of the same globalist coin) they managed to help gain them votes from 0.29% to 10% in three years. A group which is so ridiculous allegedly against the Troika but for the EU and against Merkel but for her as they condemn the protests against her. Now the corporate global media jumped on the bandwagon of GD these votes hover around 15-20%. The system is creating its next fallback option in the form of Syriza or GD as players in any coalition that might be formed.

Left unchecked illegal immigration would be a ticking time bomb. Campaigning around the fake slogan of 'migrant rights' and calling for 'unity' among all and sundry may apply to imperialist centres which had colonies all over the world but does not apply to banana republics for the scale and volume of immigration surpasses the domestic labour force (Eleftherotypia-newspaper spoke in 2004 about the presence of 2.5m so

has the Greek TUC research department INE-GSEE spoken about the presence of 40% foreign born workers in relation to the indigenous labour force). That is over a decade ago.
Campaigned pro-actively for a vote for PASOK in 1991...

Permanent Revolution ex-Workers Power (another now disbanded group and the irony here is Walters always intervenes on the scene whilst groups are on the verge of disbanding) had a blog site. I intervened initially on topics related to Greece as I did with a series of letters in Weekly Worker regarding Greece. PR forecasted perpetual boom (instead of 'catastrophist theory'... as they labelled it) just as the EZ was going into depression and they asked for a meeting and a series of eyewitness reports from Greece. In the middle of one of them when we had a two day bombardment to destroy the occupation of the squares Walters appeared with his poison pen letters (not on the content of the material which was being uploaded by the way) to talk about ....gays and immigration. PR then blocked the second eye-witness report. PR who were an offshoot of Workers Power have known that I disagree with the Americanisation of politics in fields of sexual relations (it's not the duty of labour parties to actively promote any sexual lifestyles) from the 80's. But as British they are in bed with the Yanks and kowtow to their every whim. In that they follow the political class that rules Britain to the letter. They are American poodles.

'Weekly Worker' or otherwise known as Globalist Weekly
When a book came out 'How the IMF Broke Greece' edited by me with contributions from others and was

reviewed by an ex-British miner Dave Douglass, Walters appeared on the scene (without having read it to attack it!) and to say 'illegal immigration' is good for Greece as it has been good for... America. The irony now of the situation is that illegal immigration left unchecked has led to riots in many parts of Greece. We are now being told to condemn Greeks for rioting when Greeks are being killed by the local corporate media, the foreign corporate media (Paul Mason-Newsnight Channel 4 John Snow) in other words to accept their lot as no one can go against the 4th Reich (much like the ex-cdes of the Vitsoris group) for the arrival of millions in the territory of Greece is a natural phenomena ('migration theory,' 'human rights ' in the past it was just known as Lebensraum). Funny how Cuba closes its borders to 'gusanos' but Greece cant. So why does Greece have a navy, an army and a rail service? To ship them in by the kilo dump them without any means of support in a concrete mega city and then expect them to live like hippies (ie to molest no one, to commit no crimes to live idyllically by eating air and handing out flowers to each passer by in particular old ladies not living like animals in squares and using them as latrines in 40c heat) as if they are in Matala in Crete in the 70's.

Or let's put it another way. 15 million or so tourists visit Greece a year. Why not turn the tourist industry into just a reception centre of illegal immigration so no UN conventions on 'human rights' are breached. Ensure each new arrival is housed and fed to the standard of tourists in hotels and turn Greeks into waiters for this service so they can get some hotel work back as they have been made redundant from that as well. After all an 'open border' policy espoused by Greeks who were trained under

Lyndon Larouche and happen to be the family that had the central bankster bros under Simitis who brought us into the Euro (and now pretend they are the rrrevolutionaries of Antarsya) are the direct connection between the British 'far left' and Greece.

But the fake left won't touch the topic as they don't want to go against the status quo. They are globalisations last vital bulwark. Hence when they look at Syriza they see 'success' and want to repeat it abroad as if the conditions are the same everywhere and the success of Syriza whatever that means in practice, is anything to look up to other than with the eyes of parliamentary cretins, just as the Greek parliament has ceased to exist.

There is no nationalism as yet of Greek labour. It has been decimated, de-industrialised and replaced by globalized labour which has no interest for Greece or the Greek nation. They are all there for their own individual ends not the collective ends of society as they can just up sticks and leave at any moment in time and aren't interested in society or social issues as issues. Hence one notices the total absence of immigrants from the globalist left and if they are there they are there for show like a flower on vase by the window.

But that isn't the issue with Walters. Walters does not seek debate just the closure of it by creating labels, latest one being I am David Irving when he openly supports the ethnic cleansing of Greeks. Well what label aspires to him? The only good American is a dead one? After all he is on record to not support the military conflicts arrayed against the USA from Afghanistan to Iraq... wants the mess that is the USA exported everywhere and assumes we have to fall for it.

The other irony is that all the parties of the official fake Left KKE-Syriza ask for illegals to leave Greece ie by overturning the Dublin 2 agreement and being given travel papers to go to northern Europe to alleviate Greece's problems. In other words they want Greece to be an open border arrival point, then processing and then movement up the chain. You don't hear Walters criticise them for being anti-immigration now do you? That is what Syriza and the KKE openly argue. Let's look at Lenin:

"What does 'Down with frontiers' mean? It is the beginning of anarchy.... Only when the socialist revolution has become a reality, and not a method, will the slogan 'Down with frontiers' be a correct slogan."

Lenin April 1917 on the National Question
http://classicalmarxismvsimmigration.blogspot.com/2011/02/lenin-against-open-borders.html

I remain committed to the ideals of Greece belongs to the Greeks, US Bases Out, Greece must Exit the EU etc even if Syrizas new found friends in the bankruptcy of the Anglo-American 'far left' have adopted the Brookings Institute, the London School of Economics and the world banks as their mantra and the evidence of it is that all talk of 'socialism' is in reality just talk about lifestyles (race or sex never about class). Hence there never was any 'debate' on the **WIN** site, just a concerted and united effort by Americans and their British toadies to state openly Greece should cease to exist. One does not *debate neo-fascists,* one exposes them openly for what they are, pure globalists whether of the 'open' or closed variety.

On neo-fascism...
I'll leave the last words to Lafazanis the leader of the Left Platform in Syriza with 30% of the votes at their founding conference:
"you want a procedure with Presidential decrees in order to avoid the control of Parliament – a control which is to be avoided only by non-democratic regimes. The two bourgeois parties have engineered a disgusting and to be condemned coup, blatantly, by using Parliament as a decoration"
2nd August 2013

Which leaves one with the obvious question if the Greek Parliament no longer votes on anything why does the Left still participate in it?
Answers again on a postcard please.

Much like the other question. Walters alleges he has the same line as myself on the nation state and he was criticised by Gerry (hands off the US ambassador in Libya!) Downing that he is a rabid nationalist and that a national question arises if the volume of immigration is such to question the identity of nations, but that this law is overturned if you are an imperialist country or sub-imperialist overturning Trotskys observations in 1940 that a national question may also emerge in imperialist countries if overrun by Hitler, he argues for the closure of borders in non-imperialist countries. So how come that doesn't make him a xenophobe, nationalist as Gerry alleges? So South Africa must have arrived at an imperialist level of development as well?

EU-USA=One World Govt
"The totalitarian state, subjecting all aspects of economic, political, and cultural life to finance capital, is the instrument for creating a supernationalist state, an imperialist empire, the rule over continents, the rule over the whole world."
Nationalism and Economic Life
-Leon Trotsky 1933

The centralising tendencies of global imperialism implies they no longer seek to have nation states with any role whatsoever. They are creating an imperialist unification based not on army invasions like Hitler (that happened with the defeat of Germany and Japan in WW2) but on NATO, WTO, central banks, IMF, common currencies leading to world currencies. By destroying nations or creating mini-USA's everywhere imperialism wants to create the old 'divide and rule' philosophy to control and contain all labour movements like what the British Empire did in Africa when it shipped Indians over and blocked the Blacks from working on the railways so they could not disrupt the Empire.

'Socialist' Discussion Site...
I was on the site for one month prior to withdrawing. The eyewitness report from the ERT occupation affected the Syriza lackeys... on the site. Let's have a look at some of their comments:

Greeks are 'primitive xenophobes' Dan

'Apodidactic manner' Bob Archer

After explaining to me that Greece benefitted from the EU
and EZ and the EU I am told...despite contrary information
provided from a KKE source:
'I would be grateful if vngelis would take part in the
discussion in a less strident manner.'
Dan

"The sarcasm in vngelis' postings is unpleasant and
uncomradely. S/He is constantly trying to associate those
who disagree with him as fake lefts, supporters of
quislings or appeasers of fascism. This is not an
appropriate style for this discussion"
Dan

Being labelled a terrorist here....
Both sought to "expose" the true character of the
'neofascist' state by provoking it into battles with the
revolutionary brigades; both resorted to acts of individual
terror, assassination and bomb throwing in an attempt to
short circuit the process of winning the majority of the
class. These were the Italian Red Brigades and the German
Red Army Fraction.
Dan

Sorry Comrade Gelis, I strongly disagree with your views.
If Greece is swallowed up by workers from across the
world I will not mourn but as Joe Hill put it: organize
Stu

From a primitive xenophobe to whether I am …Greek
I guess the question to Comrade Gelis and to all of us are
you Greek (or wherever you are from) first or a communist
revolutionary first? If the former than Comrade Gelis'
comments fit and present a radical nationalist view. If the
latter then we are internationalists and the borders drawn
and maintained by the oppressors mean nothing to us.
Stu

"In some ways, there is a similar issue here in California,
and we see it very concretely here in Oakland, where I
live. My own neighbourhood, for instance, used to be 90%
people born in this country; now it is a mixture of Asians,
Latin Americans, one block which is primarily Iraqis, etc.
(My own personal attitude is that this polyglot really
makes things interesting.) Yes, there is competition for
jobs. Also, I understand that some of the immigrants
receive certain government services that native born
people who are in equal need don't, and this does create
some resentment. My attitude is that everybody should get
these services.

If it is really true that Greece's economy is really, actually
being strained by the numbers of immigrants, then I think
the movement should demand that the EU help provide for
them. But what I feel most strongly is this: How can any
movement that is fighting for a better society take the
attitude towards immigrants of "You can drown in the sea.
You can go back home and be bombed to death. You can
go back home and starve." No working class movement
can take that attitude and move forward. It is inevitable
that if it does, it will turn to nationalism and some sort of
racism and/or sexism as well as homophobia, etc."

John Reinmann

"My son has worked on building sites in Greece where the lingua franca of the site was English because of the range of nationalities working there. The description of the working conditions was like something from a century ago. He is also scathing of the commonplace racism he experienced there."
Felicity Dowling (principal spokesperson of Left Unity)

Walters other American friend a lawyer Stepehen Diamond who did a stint with Healy's outfit (under Wohlforth) in the USA prior to the Greenstein mob that took over and now prints the Financial Times for the USA has ditched the Trade Unions and on the WSWS website goes round attacking the nationalism of everybody, but not the American transnational corporations that rule the world... for which Walters has defended vociferously.
"A CAPITALIST WORLD GOVERNMENT IS A UTOPIAN ILLUSION, BUT IF IT WERE IN THE OFFING, IT WOULD PROBABLY BE MORE SOMETHING TO BE WISHED FOR THAN SOMETHING TO BE FEARED. YES, I VALUE THE ELIMINATION OF WAR MUCH MORE THAN THE PRESERVATION OF GREEK NATIONAL CULTURE. YOUR VALUES ARE FUNDAMENTALLY WARPED-- IT GOES MUCH DEEPER THAN A MERE POLITICAL DIFFERENCE."
SRD

Conclusion

Even in the ex-stalinist states when the USSR was starting to collapse the old national antagonisms resurfaced. National culture, national traditions etc. re-emerged. How could that be when it was already buried as we had the creation of 'soviet man'?

To now have Americans and Brits arguing that the destruction of nation states (*under whatever guise they come up with or whatever tinpot theory they concoct*) is something progressive without the nation states volunteering to commit national hara-kiri or even allowed a vote on it, indicates how fast they have degenerated into a new world order of globalism. Anyone voicing these views (erasure of nations) should be automatically excluded, but what we see is that like 60's samizdat in the old USSR we now have a similar thing developing in the West where any views deemed 'nationalist' are banned from the *'open' 'alternative' 'anti-capitalist' 'socialist'* media outlets which are the twin side of the corporate media.

PS
Under any rules of democracy (not of course Anglo-American) one would be allowed the right of reply prior to being 'suspended' or the same rules would apply to the person who made the allegations. But of course under globalist rules all norms of basic democracy no longer apply. This indicates the *neo-fascist* nature of 'debates'. One has to first fit into a schema before being able to respond and once labelled for not answering in the pre-conceived schema one is labelled accordingly: *'anti-*

semitic' 'racist' 'homophobic' not necessarily in that order. But we don't precisely live in a democracy any more but an Orwellian new world order…As I have also other things to do than waste my time answering American provocateurs I send my reply to the allegations, but do not confirm I am willing to respond or have time to do so…

VN Gelis
August 2013

A reply to the EU's 4th Reich Empire Apologists... Weekly Worker component of British Left Unity

"If China," says Mr. Stapleton, M.P., to his constituents, "should become a great manufacturing country, I do not see how the manufacturing population of Europe could sustain the contest without descending to the level of their competitors." (Times, Sept. 3, 1873, p. 8.)

"The wished-for goal of English capital is no longer Continental wages but Chinese."

Marx

Out of the blue the known globalist rag 'Weekly Worker' regurgitates old arguments on Greece not for the sake of a discussion as they have imposed a ban on responses from myself (after the last round of ad hominem attacks by David Walters, Gerry Downing with the respect to the book produced and reviewed in Weekly Worker on Greece) (1) and have now used the services of some unknown Polish journalist to promote the EU and the American NWO.

A search on the internet finds this character but he is now deceased. Our esteemed cde. assumes a name from the past (http://en.wikipedia.org/wiki/Maciej_%C5%BBurowsk i) ...

Spitting on the past of the (19th Century) First
International and the reason Marx created it (defend
workers living standards and block the bosses ability of
recruiting workers from abroad to break strikes) he
pretends the First International didn't have whip rounds to
repatriate workers, didn't agitate against 'free movement'
and didn't realise early on that mass migration/emigration
(controlled by the bosses) led to a perpetuation of slavery.
(2) The reason he has such venum against the blog I have
is that none of it is by myself, it's what the classical
Marxists wrote and that is what enrages him as anyone can
read it and work things out for themselves.

Maciej isn't really interested in the 'debate' on open
borders. Weekly Worker is imploding and one has noticed
that they venomously allowed an attack on a Willie Hunter
(paedophile connotations) an ex-cde of theirs being an
anti-Semite (Ian Donovan) and now alleging I am a...Nazi.
These tiny outfits act as vassals to globalism to ensure the
flock return home (to Labourism) and they promote the EU
above all else (repeatedly giving to the 'permanent boom
of capitalism' lie in the letters of the buffoon Arthur
Bough).

According to John Plant (editor of Revolutionary History),
a Mike McNair was allegedly going to review the book
produced in English 'Classical Marxism and Immigration'
Edited by myself and S Lawrence (3) but presumably this
hatchet job from an anti-communist from Poland is the
answer, in other words, mass immigration is here to stay, is
positive the world over as it abolishes nation states and
leads to a...post-capitalist nirvana, which raises living

standards for the working class and does not reduce them to penury, as has happened to the Greek working class which has been forced to receive millions of illegal immigrants without being asked by the globalist Greek quisling politicians of the Fourth Reich. (Greek Cross party parliamentary committee did look into it in 1993!)(4)

In the meantime in the real world, the EU instigated expansionist wars on the borders of the EU, starting in ex-Yugoslavia and ending in the Ukraine are events that are always supported by 'WW', the 'racism' of the indigenous nationalities (Serbs, E. Ukrainians) is always decried and the hyper-globalism of the City of London/Wall St always promoted as progress, precisely because they destroy working class living standards and create a globalised 'melting pot' so beloved by an 'educated lumpen petty bourgeoisie', current shock troops of the Fourth Reich, who move abroad in search of greener pastures like they change shirts and if an 'uneducated' barbarian from the 'lower orders' dares to complain about the EU and its four core principles (freedom of movement for capital, labour, services and goods), they bring out the big hammer of 'Racism' and for those who require special treatment... 'Nazism'. No wonder the rightists are sweeping the board clean (France, UK) and there is widespread popular venom against the EU.

Maciej wants to defend his brethren in their mass movement West, (admitting by default that they are playing the role the Irish did in the Nineteenth Century in undercutting labour), but forgets to add that then capitalism was still expanding, in particular in the USA, whilst now it is declining and the jobs don't actually exist for population transfers of this gargantuan magnitude

Recent surveys have shown for example London has 200,000 less school places and the use of the ambulance service has increased by 4 million in less than a decade whilst the actual service has been cut. Is this any wonder when the new arrivals have made no contribution to the capital cost, of this infrastructure?

Characters like Maciej want their globalist (unlimited mass migration) cake with no respect for the standards of pre-existing workers or the public services they were entitled to receive. But in reality this unceasing mass immigration becomes a harbinger of the third worldisation of all standards under the guise of 'working class unity' which dictates 'don't be 'racist' show 'class solidarity' and let it happen'. There were individuals like that in WWII who argued that one could not go against the occupation soldiers of the Third Reich as they were workers like us, and they were developing unity with them, borders were being erased, we were seeing the end of 'reactionary' nation states and so on, all this bringing the struggle for 'internationalist' socialism closer. They forgot to add that in the meantime the people were experiencing barbarism and they wanted to stop it, not encourage its further spread the world over. But since 1989 the old left has made peace with capitalism and not any capitalism in general, in any particular period of history, but US capitalism, the last global capitalism (that has used nuclear weapons and has the power to self-destruct) and it is to this type of capitalism, the bastard offspring of European capitalism, we must all bow down to.

The American Empire inaugurating its NWO destroyed the multi-ethnic state of ex-Yugoslavia in cahoots with German imperialism. Now it is intent on destroying the old nation states of Europe with the mass importation of millions of illegal immigrants, one of which is Maciej himself. Some E European countries, like Albania, haven't even joined, but their population was one of the first into the EU. No host countries were allowed a referendum on the entrance of E Europe. This process has created multi-ethnic ghettos with no tradition and no history. In the field of labour we have had the emergence of zero hours contracts, the equivalent of these multi-ethnic entities could be characterised as 'zero history nations'. To this Maciej subscribes politically, but of course someone from 'WW' didn't tell him that he joined the 'party' just as it finished... (Lehman's bros crash)

Stalinism, a cancer of the labour movement for a whole historical period, allowed the collapse of the British Empire to morph into the American one and get away scot free. Today the practitioners of the politics of globalism are everywhere defending and promoting America in decline, but nowhere more so than decrepit British Labourism and the trade union flunkeys that fund it and have made its politics indistinguishable from the Texas oil-igarchy.

On the other allegations which are the stock in trade of American globalists that there is only one holocaust ie the jewish one, (no Russian or Black or Armenian one) this obviously fits in with the adoption of cold war politics which sought to minimise the intra-european nature of WW2 (ie Russian, Greek resistance as a % of total population dead and in overall numbers) and elevate American storytelling that WW2 was only about the …jews and if anyone was to question that they would join the ranks …of 'holocaust deniers'. This type of garbage works well in academia or the 'legal marxists' (as Lenin referred to them in his days), but in the real world people just laugh. For deep down it's the politics of Hollywood, praising the US Empire even when we all know it can't fight (Vietnam, Iraq Afghanistan) or it joins wars right at the end to come on top (WW1 and WW2). Especially when we have current war criminals going about the business (Blair, Bush etc.)

Why the sudden interest in Greece? When Greece officially defaults and goes back to its national currency the whole EU project which was a political attempt at unifying the ruling classes will start to fully unravel. It is this event and this fact alone that massively enrages the pettybourgeoisie and they focus all their energies in arguing 'Greeks should be erased from history' (David Walters) (5) if that is to save the EU and condemning the nationalism of the Greeks (whilst at the same time defending the supra-nationalism of the EU, NATO, USA) or the hyper nationalism of the Germans (whose sole claim to fame is that they bankrupt Europe time after time). The Pole Maciej is in good company. Having abandoned Russia and slavish subservience to Stalinism he has gone over direct from Warsaw without a stop straight to Washington and embraced globalism fully. If he was to be a waiter or even a doorman at the top table one could say good luck and good riddance, but I doubt if they ever even assign him a role in taking out the garbage, for which he has been trained (when he throws Weekly Worker into his own)…

For after all a so-called paper that prints attacks, but bars the right to reply is nothing better than the Murdoch press, a print medium they have more in common than anyone else. (6)

Part Two:

Who runs Weekly Worker? Grandson of Neville Chamberlain ex-PM and Grandfater Secretary of State for Colonies?

That would explain why they are so pro-EU. They want it to reach New Delhi (Mode 4 agreement as highlighted by No2EU) and recreate the 19th Century Empire all over, not only does this run in their politics, it presumably runs in their veins...

VN Gelis

Notes

1. Dave Douglass Review of How the IMF Broke Greece: Eyewitness Reports and the Rold of the Fake Left

http://imfoccupationgreece.blogspot.co.uk/2011/12/dave-douglass-reviews-vn-gelis-how-imf.html

2. http://classicalmarxismvsimmigration.blogspot.co.uk/

3. Book on Classical Marxism and Immigration

http://classicalmarxismvsimmigration.blogspot.co.uk/20
12/10/coming-soon-new-book-on-immigration.html

4. The Left knew: Cross Party Parliamentary
Committee on the Impact of Mass Immigration

http://imfoccupationgreece.blogspot.co.uk/2013/08/
the-left-knewparliamentary-committee-on.html

5. David Walters: An American Provocateur Proponent
of One World Government..

http://imfoccupationgreece.blogspot.co.uk/2013/11/briti
sh-american-globalist-fake.html

6. Unpublished Letter to Weekly Worker

http://imfoccupationgreece.blogspot.co.uk/2012/02/unp
ublished-letter-to-weekly-worker.html

http://derekthomas2010.wordpress.com/2013/03/01/
who-is-richard-seymours-friend-john-chamberlain/

Bibliography

*With **special thanks** to the following websites/individuals.
It has to be noted that there **are a range of views** in this
book and not all the participants either agree with each
others views or do I agree with all their views, but they are
presented so a foreign audience can get a better picture of
the situation in Greece.*

Video Interview of Takis Fotopoulos
https://www.youtube.com/watch?v=Es8jU3dSgyo

Takis Fotopoulos
http://www.inclusivedemocracy.org/journal/

James Petras http://petras.lahaine.org/

Tartatovsky www.truthout.org

Venezuela
Leo Garib reporter from Venezuelan Press

Karamihas PASEGES Agricultural Coops Greece

Books by VN Gelis

How the IMF Broke Greece

The Greek Civil War

Syriza: Neoliberals in Disguise

Greece: Revolutionary History

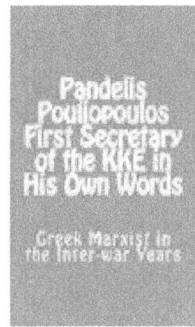

KKE First Secretary P Pouliopoulos

Classic Marxists Texts on Immigration

Third World Traveller

Websites

http://imfoccupationgreece.blogspot.co.uk/

http://patari.org/